MW01716893

God Blog Meditations

Twenty Weeks of Walking with Jesus

By Susan M. Provost

PublishAmerica
Baltimore

© 2010 by Susan M. Provost
All rights reserved. No part of this book may be reproduced, stored in a retrieval system or transmitted in any form or by any means without the prior written permission of the publishers, except by a reviewer who may quote brief passages in a review to be printed in a newspaper, magazine or journal.

First printing

PublishAmerica has allowed this work to remain exactly as the author intended, verbatim, without editorial input.

Hardcover 978-1-4512-3620-0
Softcover 978-1-4512-3619-4
PAperback 978-1-4512-5948-3
PUBLISHED BY PUBLISHAMERICA, LLLP
www.publishamerica.com
Baltimore

Printed in the United States of America

Dedication

We never end our spiritual journey in this life. Life happens, and sometimes what happens is not easy to take. What makes life easier for me is to know that I am not alone. No matter what happens, I have love, acceptance, and compassion given to me by Jesus. Spirituality grows in me as I connect with the God who loves me. My desire is to share my understanding of love with others, so they can experience what I have found in my own relationship with God. Therefore, I dedicate this book to Jesus and all those who love Jesus, especially my husband, Joe.

PREFACE

How do we know that Jesus is the Christ?

The Empty Tomb—Was it empty?

The empty tomb was a subject especially noted by the Apostle John. In the 20th chapter of his account, John describes himself as the "other disciple" who ran ahead of Peter and reached the tomb first. Looking in, John saw "the strips of linen lying there" which had been the wrappings of Jesus' dead body (verse 6). He describes, also, that the burial cloth, which had been around Jesus' head, was "folded up by itself, separate from the linen" (verse 7).

John's description of the empty tomb gives details that are evidence of an eyewitness account. These were details that convinced John, himself, because he explains, "He saw and believed" (verse 8). The small detail of the face cloth lying separate and folded implies the recognition of a deliberate, careful action. Inasmuch as Christ's body received life, He awoke and deliberately removed the cloth, folded it, and set it aside. John, the beloved disciple, recognized the simple details and thought them worthy of specific report.

Was the tomb entirely empty? No! Evidence remained of a living Christ, a risen Lord. The significance extends further, yet. Because the tomb was empty and Christ was raised to life in the body, believers count on the promise of a like glorious body. "Who by the power that enables him to bring everything under his control, will transform our lowly bodies so that they will be like his glorious body" (Philippians 3:21).

A body that defeats death and the curse of death is the inheritance of every believer. "And if the Spirit of him who raised Christ from the dead is living in you, he who raised Christ from the dead will also give life to your mortal bodies through His Spirit who lives in you" (Romans 8:11). The completion of salvation through Jesus Christ is to be saved entirely, so that even the body is immortal through "the power of an indestructible life" (Hebrews 7:16, 25). Even now, "we wait eagerly for our adoption as sons, the redemption of our bodies" (Romans 8:23).

Was the tomb empty? No! It held the evidence of life from the dead—the hope of every believer. In that hope the Christian lives each day, though he may experience trials and hardship. Paul said, "We always carry about in our body the death of Jesus, so that the life of Jesus may be revealed in our body" (2 Corinthians 4:10).

Therefore, have hope and believe in Jesus the Risen Christ. He has paved the way for us to someday experience our own empty tomb as we share the eternal life he promised to us.

Introduction

Why did I write this book of meditations?

I never thought that I would be posting a blog let alone publishing a book of blogs. I am not one to put personal information on the internet. However, someone suggested that I post a blog about something that I am passionate about. That made it easy. I am passionate about my belief and faith in Jesus. In December of 2009, in a ceremony attended by my husband, children, and grandchildren, I received my Masters Degree in Spiritual Formation and Leadership. Spirituality and relationship with Jesus is the focus of my degree and my life. It is my desire that my God blogs will bring a little of my experience of Jesus to those out there who may be searching for meaning in their lives.

The essence of spirituality is the sense of knowing that God loves us. We must know this not only in our heads, but also in our hearts and in our everyday lives. God loves us so much that God sent God's only son, Jesus, to die for us in atonement for our sins. God's love was not determined by our actions, but on how much God loved us. God loves us first and it is our quest to discover how through God's love we can be transformed into vessels of love that God pours out to our world.

Always remember that God loves you.

Week 1-Monday

Who is God?

"I am the Alpha and the Omega—the beginning and the end," says the Lord God. "I am the one who is, who always was, and who is still to come—the Almighty One."

(Revelation 1:8)

Does God love us?

"For God so loved the world that he gave his one and only Son, that whoever believes in him shall not perish but have eternal life. For God did not send his Son into the world to condemn the world, but to save the world through him (John 3:16-17).

"This is how God showed his love among us: He sent his one and only Son into the world that we might live through him. This is love: not that we loved God, but that he loved us and sent his Son as an atoning sacrifice for our sins" (1 John 4:9-10).

Why does God love us?

26 *Then God said, "Let us make man in our image, in our likeness,*
and let them rule over the fish of the sea and the birds of the air, over
the livestock, over all the earth,[1] *and over all the creatures that move*
along the ground."

27 *So God created man in his own image,*
in the image of God he created him;
male and female he created them.

28 *God blessed them and said to them, "Be fruitful and increase in*
number; fill the earth and subdue it. Rule over the fish of the sea and the
birds of the air and over every living creature that moves on the
ground."

29 *Then God said, "I give you every seed-bearing plant on the face*
of the whole earth and every tree that has fruit with seed in it. They will
be yours for food. 30 *And to all the beasts of the earth and all the birds*
of the air and all the creatures that move on the ground—everything

that has the breath of life in it—I give every green plant for food." And it was so.

[31] God saw all that he had made, and it was very good." (Genesis 1:26-31)

God is the father/mother of creation. God is our eternal parent. God loves us because God chose to create us. We are God's children. Just as good parents, we want our children to have all that we can give them. God wants to give us all that is good. Just as we want our children to know who we are, so God wants us to know who God is. We want to communicate our love for our children; God also wants to communicate God's love for us. God desires a relationship with us, as does any good parent wants to have a relationship with their children.

The problem:

We are able to see our parents in the flesh. We do not see God in the flesh. Even though Jesus became one of us to display in the flesh God's love for us, we do not see Jesus in the flesh today.

The solution:

What we know today of God, we know through faith. We trust in God's goodness because we can see the beauty of God's creation. We can also see the beauty of God in each other. We are all creations of God and God wants us to know how much God loves us. To feel the warmth of God's love, we must open ourselves (just a little) so that God can take hold of our hearts and help us understand the depth of God's love. God will help us if only we ask.

Week 1-Tuesday

God is always with us.

Every day is a gift from God. We can spend the day disliking what we do. We can spend the day being angry and hurt, sad and alone. We can do that if that is what we want to do. Instead, I prefer to spend the day looking at all the good that has occurred in my life. I lost my job last October, but I did not lose my husband, children or grandchildren. I lost my job, but I did not lose the love God has for me. I lost my job, but I am still alive and able to find something else to work at. I lost my job, but I did not lose heart, because I knew that God was with me. I lost my job, but did not lose what was important to me, my faith. There is always a plan that God has for us, but sometimes a door has to close for another door to open.

Each of us needs to fully grasp and understand just how much God loves us. We need to see how He is intimately concerned about every single detail of our lives. Reading that God loves us in His Word and understanding that He died for our sins, can still be merely intellectual pursuits. However, receiving His Spirit and experiencing His Life in and through us, is something we can never deny as being ultimate, personal love. However, the way in which to feel that ultimate personal love is not readily apparent to us.

Unfortunately, our culture encourages the need to be constantly in motion. We have the need to be productive and fill all our time with something. We become nervous when we encounter empty space, when there is a gap in a conversation, when we do not know what to say, when we are sitting in a waiting room and there are no magazines on the table to read. For most people, just doing nothing is unthinkable.

It can be difficult to encounter God while the focus of our lives is on the importance of earthly power and possessions. We cannot notice God working in our lives when we do not take the time to stop and notice anything. We do not know how to step out of the world of progress. We are moving so fast through our lives that we take no time to notice what is happening around us when the noticing is not necessary to fulfill our goal. In essence, we are programmed not to accept who we are, but we are driven to judge others and ourselves by earthly success, productivity, and accumulation of things. Consequently, we have no real appreciation for others or ourselves. We are trapped in a jail of our own creation.

Move out of your own jail and find out what it is God wants you to do. You may already be doing it, or you may need to leave something in order to do it. Do not be sorrowful. God is with you.

Week 1-Wednesday

How do you meet God?

I realize every day that God is not out there in space waiting to snatch us at death. God is an active God. God is with me every day as I go through my daily life. God is there, but I must make the effort to see God.

It can be difficult to encounter God while the focus of our lives is on the importance of earthly power and possessions. We cannot notice God working in our lives when we do not take the time to stop and notice anything. We do not know how to step out of the world of progress. We are moving so fast through our lives that we take no time to notice what is happening around us when the noticing is not necessary to fulfill our goal. In essence, we are programmed not to accept who we are, but we are driven to judge others and ourselves by earthly success, productivity, and accumulation of things. Consequently, we have no real appreciation for others or ourselves. We are trapped in a jail of our own creation.

At some point, we discover that these goals of success, productivity, and the constant drive to acquire things do not fill or satisfy the soul within us. We burn out from what has become a road to spiritual death. We look for someone to convince us that we are of value for who we really are, not what we and our culture chooses to label us. We look for someone who we do not have to prove that we are worth something. We look to connect with the Creator, the Savior, and the Spirit of the God who loves us. Our soul yearns to make that connection and to feel whole, to feel significant, and to feel loved. We may search, but we have not learned how to make this connection. Have you seen God today?

Week 1-Thursday

Does life really work for you?

28 One of the teachers of the law came and heard them debating. Noticing
that Jesus had given them a good answer, he asked him, "Of all the
commandments, which is the most important?"

29 "The most important one," answered Jesus, "is this: 'Hear, O Israel,
the Lord our God, the Lord is one.] 30 Love the Lord your God with all your
heart and with all your soul and with all your mind and with all your
strength.' [f] 31 The second is this: 'Love your neighbor as yourself.' There is
no commandment greater than these."

32 "Well said, teacher," the man replied. "You are right in saying that God
is one and there is no other but him. 33 To love him with all your heart, with
all your understanding and with all your strength, and to love your neighbor
as yourself is more important than all burnt offerings and sacrifices."

34 When Jesus saw that he had answered wisely, he said to him, "You are
not far from the kingdom of God." And from then on no one dared ask him
any more questions. (Mark 12:28-34)

Do you feel you need something more in your life? Are you looking for a spirituality that will give your life purpose?

Through Christian spirituality, Jesus speaks to our darkness with His eternal message of love. We all long for true spiritual connections that transcend our hurried existence and from which we can leave our world of the temporary and changeable and secure a sense of the permanent and unchangeable. We can only receive this security by developing our relationship with Jesus.

Security will not come from a new age therapy, from the accumulation of wealth, nor from any of our earthly relationships. We must come to Jesus, embracing our spiritual bankruptcy and brokenness, and seeking His love and acceptance. He is continually reaching out to us, waiting for us to finally acknowledge Him and recognize His presence in our lives. Christian spirituality is ultimately about love, service to others and selflessness. Try Jesus, you may just like his message.

Week 1-Friday

The Question of the Day : How do you know God is near?

[16]Then the eleven disciples went to Galilee, to the mountain where Jesus had told them to go. [17]When they saw him, they worshiped him; but some doubted. [18]Then Jesus came to them and said, "All authority in heaven and on earth has been given to me. [19]Therefore go and make disciples of all nations, baptizing them in[l] the name of the Father and of the Son and of the Holy Spirit, [20]and teaching them to obey everything I have commanded you. And surely I am with you always, to the very end of the age." (Matthew 28: 16-20)

How do you know that God is near? On the other hand, if you do not think he is near, where do you think he is?

We do not need to find God; we only need to recognize that God is already in our lives. God is continually working in our lives, but many of us do not feel or see this work. What is offered is the humble quest of a God who, in the person of Jesus, comes to reveal His love and beg our love in return. Communication with God is essential, just as it is in any relationship. Communication is how we make the connection and build our human relationships; we learn to connect the same way with God through the communication called prayer.

Communication is not so much what we have to give God, but is more a living with God, a meeting with one who loves us unconditionally, a personal relationship in which it is truly God who does the giving, the giving of himself for us. The experience of being fully present in this personal relationship with God could be described as an altered state of awareness.

Each of us needs to fully grasp and understand just how much we are loved by God. Because of his love for us, God is intimately concerned about every aspect of our lives. We cannot just acknowledge God intellectually, but we must feel his loving presence. We must acknowledge his presence within us, and understand the sacrifice he made in dying on the cross in order to demonstrate the extent of his great love.

Week 1-Saturday

Everyday there is an Opportunity to Meet God

[18]A certain ruler asked him, "Good teacher, what must I do to inherit eternal life?"

[19]"Why do you call me good?" Jesus answered. "No one is good—except God alone. [20]You know the commandments: 'Do not commit adultery, do not murder, do not steal, do not give false testimony, honor your father and mother.'[b]"

[21]"All these I have kept since I was a boy," he said.

[22]When Jesus heard this, he said to him, "You still lack one thing. Sell everything you have and give to the poor, and you will have treasure in heaven. Then come, follow me."

[23]When he heard this, he became very sad, because he was a man of great wealth. [24]Jesus looked at him and said, "How hard it is for the rich to enter the kingdom of God! [25]Indeed, it is easier for a camel to go through the eye of a needle than for a rich man to enter the kingdom of God."

[26]Those who heard this asked, "Who then can be saved?"

[27]Jesus replied, "What is impossible with men is possible with God."

[28]Peter said to him, "We have left all we had to follow you!"

[29]"I tell you the truth," Jesus said to them, "no one who has left home or wife or brothers or parents or children for the sake of the kingdom of God [30]will fail to receive many times as much in this age and, in the age to come, eternal life." (Luke 18:18-29)

God knows you best. He created you, uniquely. It is not likely that Jesus is going to walk up to you as he did to the apostles and say directly, "Come, follow me." Instead, God will guide you through prayer and experiences. Pray quietly, pray often, "God, what do you want me to do with my life?"

Prayer for Vocation
Almighty and eternal God,
in your unfailing love you provide
many blessings to all who serve you.
We pray for the ears to hear
the call to serve the Church of Jesus

Inspire us to a generous response.
Grant us courage and vision to
serve your people.
May our lives and service call your
people to respond to the presence
of your Spirit among us
that, faithful to the Gospel and
hope of Jesus the Christ, we may: announce glad tidings to the poor
proclaim liberty to captives,
set prisoners free
and renew the face of the earth.

O God, Father of all Mercies, Provider of a bountiful Harvest, send Your Graces upon us who you have called to gather the fruits of your labor; preserve and strengthen them in their lifelong service of you.

Open the hearts of your children that we may discern Your Holy Will; inspire in us a love and desire to surrender ourselves to serving others in the name of your son, Jesus Christ.

Teach us all to follow our respective paths in life guided by Your Divine Word and Truth. Through the intercession of the Most Blessed Virgin Mary, all the Angels, and Saints, humbly hear our prayers and grant Your Church's needs, through Christ, our Lord. Amen.

Week 1-Sunday

Jesus came to heal us

[16]I am not ashamed of the gospel, because it is the power of God for the salvation of everyone who believes: first for the Jew, then for the Gentile. [17]For in the gospel a righteousness from God is revealed, a righteousness that is by faith from first to last, just as it is written: "The righteous will live by faith."

(Romans 1:16-17)

[35]That day when evening came, he said to his disciples, "Let us go over to the other side." [36]Leaving the crowd behind, they took him along, just as he was, in the boat. There were also other boats with him. [37]A furious squall came up, and the waves broke over the boat, so that it was nearly swamped. [38]Jesus was in the stern, sleeping on a cushion. The disciples woke him and said to him, "Teacher, don't you care if we drown?"

[39]He got up, rebuked the wind and said to the waves, "Quiet! Be still!" Then the wind died down and it was completely calm.

[40]He said to his disciples, "Why are you so afraid? Do you still have no faith?"

[41]They were terrified and asked each other, "Who is this? Even the wind and the waves obey him!"

(Mark 4:35-41)

Jesus came to bring us the good news of salvation. However, what does salvation mean? Throughout the New Testament, the words "save," "saved," and "salvation" have their root in the Greek "sozo" which means to save, to rescue, to deliver, to protect. "Sozo" is also translated in the New Testament with the words heal, preserve, save, do well, and to make whole. The Greek "soteria" (which has its origin in "sozo") is the main word translated "salvation." "Soteria" is also translated to deliver, health, salvation, save and saving.

One can learn the full meaning of a Greek word by studying the scriptures where it is used and the way it is interpreted. You can easily see from the previous definitions that "salvation" means much more than a soul's preparation for Heaven. In Romans 1:16-17, the Apostle

Paul writes, "For I am not ashamed of the gospel of Christ; for it is the power of God for salvation ("soteria") to everyone that believes...For there is the righteousness of God revealed from faith to faith."

Jesus came to bring us salvation, which means He came to rescue, deliver, protect, heal, and save us. He came to make us whole and to reconnect us with the God who loves us. He came so save us from our sin, our despair, our loneliness, our fear and our lack of faith (Mark 4:35-41).

Week 2-Monday

What is Christian Spirituality?

Then Jesus went around teaching from village to village. [7]Calling the Twelve to him, he sent them out two by two and gave them authority over evil spirits.

[8]These were his instructions: "Take nothing for the journey except a staff—no bread, no bag, no money in your belts. [9]Wear sandals but not an extra tunic. [10]Whenever you enter a house, stay there until you leave that town. [11]And if any place will not welcome you or listen to you, shake the dust off your feet when you leave, as a testimony against them."

[12]They went out and preached that people should repent. [13]They drove out many demons and anointed many sick people with oil and healed them. (Mark 6:6:13)

Christian spirituality describes the whole of the Christian's life. Christian spirituality is an orientation to self-transcending knowledge, freedom, and love. It will illuminate our ultimate values and highest ideals perceived and pursued in the mystery of Jesus Christ through the Holy Spirit in the Church and practiced in the community of disciples. That is to say, spirituality is concerned with everything that constitutes the Christian experience. It is concerned specifically with the perception and pursuit of the highest ideal or goal of Christian life, which is an ever more intense union with God disclosed in Christ through life in the Spirit.

Christianity Spirituality is the quest for a fulfilled and authentic life. It involves taking the beliefs and values of Christianity and weaving them into the fabric of our lives, so that they animate, provide the breath, spirit, and fire for our lives. Christian spirituality is the desire to live our lives following the example of Jesus Christ. We are to live a life constituting selfless love, compassion, and forgiveness. Christian spirituality is expressed in the community of the faithful because to be truly Christian requires a relationship with God and with others in God's family.

Christian spirituality is the way to internalize the message of Christ, so that we live it out in our own journey. Experience has taught us that in this life there is no absolute security or lasting peace. It is important to remember that our security can only be found in trusting Christ with all we have and all that we are, being certain that He will never fail us. It is our participation in the life of God, and the model for the way in which each of us listens for his work.

Through Christian spirituality, we come to know that we are lovable persons and that God loves us at this moment and accepts us as we are. We discover that Christ is not just a historical figure, but also one who lives with us continually. We learn to let go of whatever prevents us from entering into a life of perfect freedom in Christ.

Week 2-Tuesday

How shall we live?

[25] *"Though I have been speaking figuratively, a time is coming when I will no longer use this kind of language but will tell you plainly about my Father.* [26] *In that day you will ask in my name. I am not saying that I will ask the Father on your behalf.* [27] *No, the Father himself loves you because you have loved me and have believed that I came from God.* [28] *I came from the Father and entered the world; now I am leaving the world and going back to the Father."* (John 16:25-28)

How Jesus lived his own life as a human shows how we are to live ours (John 16:25-28). In his own life, Jesus lived simply. He was deeply in love with everything and everyone living, from God down to the simplest creature. He was gentle and compassionate, especially to those who were ostracized by society. He never gave an appearance of self-righteousness, but had a genuine humility and meekness and an understanding of others.

It is revealing that Jesus chose a wedding party for the launch of His public ministry. The news of what he did probably spread like wildfire, alerting everyone in the surrounding area to His kindness and His remarkable gift to the bride and groom. Kindness seems to be the message that Jesus wanted to precede Him, to disarm people so that they would not fear Him. Everything about Jesus spoke of simplicity, being born in a stable, living an unknown existence, showing nothing out of the ordinary except when some need called forth His extraordinary power to heal or to comfort.

It did not take long before this simple preacher aroused the hostility of the religious leaders. It is very strange how they could feel so threatened by a Person who preached only the highest of ideals and spent His days comforting and healing, and His nights in prayer. Jesus, however, did not allow Himself to become obsessed with their criticisms and harassment. He concerned Himself with relationships, with His Father and with the people. Jesus said to love one another.

He also said that the kingdom of God is here! We are called to live in God's kingdom now. Why does Christ's teaching seem so confusing? It is confusing because His message was not merely aimed at conveying information. It sought to precipitate something more important: the spiritual transformation of the hearers. Transformation comes about through relationship. God's actions came about due to a desire to be in relationship. God loves us and wants to be in relationship with us. What a blessed thing!

Week 2-Wednesday

We are not self-sufficient.

He was praying in a certain place, and when he ceased, one of his disciples said to him, "Lord, teach us to pray, as John taught his disciples." And he said to them, "When you pray, say:

'Father, hallowed be thy name. Thy kingdom come. Give us each day our daily bread; and forgive us our sins, for we ourselves forgive every one who is indebted to us; and lead us not into temptation"' [Luke 11:1-4].

Spirituality is the quest for a connection with God, the Divine Creator, or the higher power that put us here. Spirituality is a lifelong journey that cannot find completion until we leave this life and attain full communion with the deity of our quest. Prayer is an important way that we construct this relationship with God or higher power. We all think that we know how to talk to God, but we do not always know how to listen to him. My spiritual journey has taken me from a reliance on self to awareness that self is not sufficient. It has taken me from a belief that success is related to power and acquisition to the knowledge that success is related to my connection with God and knowing that everything good comes from God.

Life is a journey and we are all travelers. The spiritual journey is a quest to find the meaning to life, the secrets of creation, or to connect with the higher power that put us here. My spiritual journey has put me on a road that has taken me from the depths of despair and desolation to the heights of joy and fulfillment. I have not found God, because he was not lost, but I have found my path to God. God had been patiently waiting for me to allow him to lead me and in the passage of time, I have become trusting enough to allow him to do so.

Week 2-Thursday

Is Jesus looking for you?

"3Then Jesus told them this parable: 4"Suppose one of you has a hundred sheep and loses one of them. Does he not leave the ninety-nine in the open country and go after the lost sheep until he finds it? 5And when he finds it, he joyfully puts it on his shoulders 6and goes home. Then he calls his friends and neighbors together and says, 'Rejoice with me; I have found my lost sheep.' 7I tell you that in the same way there will be more rejoicing in heaven over one sinner who repents than over ninety-nine righteous persons who do not need to repent. (Luke 15:3-7)

We have heard this parable many times and we think that we know what it means. Do you really believe that a good shepherd will leave 99 sheep to search for one? In reality that sounds pretty stupid. Because if he goes to find one sheep, the 99 sheep will scatter because they have no leader. The will be eaten by wolves with no one to protect them. It is not sound business sense to go after one. The good shepherd in this case will cut his losses and pay closer attention to the 99 so he won't lose any more.

Jesus was not just talking about any good shepherd. Jesus was talking about himself. Jesus is not happy if even one of his flock (us) gets lost. Because Jesus loves each one of us, he will look for his lost sheep until he can bring them back into the fold. Jesus does not cut his losses, and concentrate his efforts on the 99 who did not get away. He will look for us and call to us until he finds us. He will not stop, he will not let one of his sheep stay lost. When he hears us cry out, he will come to get us, where we are. We don't even have to go to him, he will come to us because of his great love for us. And he celebrates that his lost sheep was found.

Are you lost? Call out to Jesus and he will come and care for you.

Week 2-Friday

Have Confidence before God

"21Dear friends, if our hearts do not condemn us, we have confidence before God 22and receive from him anything we ask, because we obey his commands and do what pleases him. 23And this is his command: to believe in the name of his Son, Jesus Christ, and to love one another as he commanded us. 24Those who obey his commands live in him, and he in them. And this is how we know that he lives in us: We know it by the Spirit he gave us".

(1 John 3:21-24)

Confidence is another way of saying we have assurance before God. There is a purpose for this confidence. We cannot appropriate the promises of God if we are not assured of something when we ask. We have to ask with confidence, and we can only do that when we are in line with God's will.

God's precious promises will not fall on us automatically. We have to know the will of God before we can even ask for them. We have to ask in line with His will. God's Word is God's will. Many people say things like, well, if God wants me to have something He will just give it to me. This is not scriptural and can cause problems for us and get us discouraged.

There is a purpose to everything God does and says. He wants us to be confident in our asking so we can appropriate His promises. He wouldn't have given us promises if He didn't want us to have them would He? Yet, he wants us to grow up into maturity so that we can not only receive the promises but use these promised blessings to be a blessing to others.

Another way of saying this would be to say, we can have confidence when we ask God for something that is according to his will, and because we have confidence in what we are asking for, we know we are going to receive what we asked for. We can say this because our desires are in line with His desires. We are asking for what He told us to ask for. We are asking for His will. This may seem over simplistic but I believe many people miss this important truth and fall short, never knowing where they missed it.

Pray confidently before God, because that is what God wants from his beloved children. We must pray to always want what God's will is for us. God knows what we need and what will be good for us mentally, spiritually and physically. We must have confidence that God's loving will for us will bring us true happiness.

Week 2-Saturday

An Attitude of Gratitude

1 The LORD reigns,
let the nations tremble;
he sits enthroned between the cherubim,
let the earth shake.

2 Great is the LORD in Zion;
he is exalted over all the nations.

3 Let them praise your great and awesome name—
he is holy.

4 The King is mighty, he loves justice—
you have established equity;
in Jacob you have done
what is just and right.

5 Exalt the LORD our God
and worship at his footstool;
he is holy.

6 Moses and Aaron were among his priests,
Samuel was among those who called on his name;
they called on the LORD
and he answered them.

7 He spoke to them from the pillar of cloud;
they kept his statutes and the decrees he gave them.

8 O LORD our God,
you answered them;
you were to Israel a forgiving God,

though you punished their misdeeds.

[9] Exalt the LORD our God
and worship at his holy mountain,
for the LORD our God is holy.
(Psalm 99)

God has been very good to me. I am grateful for all the wonderful things that God has given me. It is so easy to become negative and focus on things that are going wrong. You have to develop a habit of looking at the bright side of things, things you can be grateful about. I realize that I have been very blessed in my life with family and friends that I love to spend time with.

It is easy to find fault with everything and everyone especially when things do not seem to be going our way. However, don't you know people who are always happy? They can be very annoying, can't they? Always looking on the bright side, always looking for the positive. These people also seem to be happy most all of the time.

Getting into the habit of being positive and grateful can also make for a happier person. You probably also know of someone who is always negative, always going through some type of disaster. There is always something wrong with their lives. They also seem to be very unhappy

people. God has given us such a beautiful world. We just need to recognize it and be grateful for it.

It is worth a try, anyway.

Week 2-Sunday

If it does no harm, let it go.

[38] *"You have heard that it was said, 'Eye for eye, and tooth for tooth. [39] But I tell you, do not resist an evil person. If someone strikes you on the right cheek, turn to him the other also. [40] And if someone wants to sue you and take your tunic let him have your cloak as well. [41] If someone forces you to go one mile, go with him two miles. [42] Give to the one who asks you, and do not turn away from the one who wants to borrow from you.*

[43] *"You have heard that it was said, 'Love your neighbor and hate your enemy.' [44] But I tell you: Love your enemies and pray for those who persecute you, [45] that you may be sons of your Father in heaven. He causes his sun to rise on the evil and the good, and sends rain on the righteous and the unrighteous. [46] If you love those who love you, what reward will you get? Are not even the tax collectors doing that? [47] And if you greet only your brothers, what are you doing more than others? Do not even pagans do that? [48] Be perfect, therefore, as your heavenly Father is perfect. (Matthew 5:38-50)*

I was talking with someone who works with Alzheimer's patients and in dealing with them; she learned that "if it does no harm, let it go."

Now what does that mean? The literal version in the world of the Alzheimer patient means that if they are not doing something that will actually hurt them or others, do not get so worried about correcting it. In my heart, I believe that God is looking at us in the same way.

How can that advice be used in my daily life? Can I get stuck with getting angry over a toilet seat being left up? The act of leaving the toilet seat up does no harm. Do I get mad if the toothpaste is squeezed down the center and not curled up, as I would like it? The act of squeezing the toothpaste does no harm. Do I blow up if a glass is not put into the dishwasher, but left on the counter? The act of leaving a glass on the counter does no harm.

I guess what I am saying is that we have to treat each other with the same kindness that we would if someone were ill. The person you jump on and criticize could be someone that you love and yet you are not going to let him or her get away with doing anything that you think should not be done or criticize the way they handle a task. This to me really goes hand in hand with having an understanding of what it means to show forgiveness. When we forgive, we have to let it go and move on. Sometimes letting it go is very difficult. We feel we must have things our way or we feel that it is the wrong way. Our way is not always the correct "highway."

However, as Christians we should always be looking at ourselves, examining our actions, correcting our thoughts so that they are more in line with what Jesus would think or feel or say. "What Would Jesus Do?" should be our mantra. This entails thinking and living with love, compassion, and forgiveness as the leading factors of how we behave. Your focus should not be about what someone has "done to you," but instead of what you might have "done to others." Taking on the mind and heart of Jesus is the call of all Christians. It is a moving away from the selfish and moving toward the self-less.

Week 3-Monday

What is important to you?

[13]Someone in the crowd said to him, "Teacher, tell my brother to divide the inheritance with me."

[14]Jesus replied, "Man, who appointed me a judge or an arbiter between you?" [15]Then he said to them, "Watch out! Be on your guard against all kinds of greed; a man's life does not consist in the abundance of his possessions."

[16]And he told them this parable: "The ground of a certain rich man produced a good crop. [17]He thought to himself, 'What shall I do? I have no place to store my crops.'

[18]"Then he said, 'This is what I'll do. I will tear down my barns and build bigger ones, and there I will store all my grain and my goods. [19]And I'll say to myself, "You have plenty of good things laid up for many years. Take life easy; eat, drink and be merry."'

[20]"But God said to him, 'You fool! This very night your life will be demanded from you. Then who will get what you have prepared for yourself?'

[21]"This is how it will be with anyone who stores up things for himself but is not rich toward God."

(Luke 12:13-21)

We all have time for people and activities that we find important. When I hear someone say, "I don't have time" or "I am too busy," I think that they are really saying, "This is not important to me." It is good to be able to draw the line and limit the activities that erupt during day. We all are drawn into far too many activities. We have too many people who want our time.

So, what is important? I used to say that my job was important. I worked many more hours than was necessary in the name of taking care of what is important. I probably sacrificed family, friends, and especially God in my misdirection of what was important. True, you have to have money in order to live. Food, clothing, and shelter all cost money. However, how much do you need?

When I lost my job, I discovered that the job was not important. The love of family and friends, those who took the time to be with me during my time of trouble, they were important. The loss of a job just limited my ability to spend. The loss of any of these people in my life, who have been and are there for me, would truly be tragic. They are important

In addition, while I was trying to find happiness in things, I completely forgot the one who is with me during all the times of my life. I neglected the one who would never let me down and the one who asks for so little and gives so much. I forgot about my true friend. The great thing is that Jesus was still there when I finally decided to look at what was important in my life. He did not turn away from me, when I turned away from him. I had no time for him and his people, but that did not stop his giving love to me.

I was one of those people who did not have time to spend with God. My life was too busy. I had more important things to do, or so I thought. The greatest gift in my life is realizing that God always has time for me. He is never too busy to help me during my times of sorrow and celebrate with me during my time of great happiness. He is there for all of us and is never too busy to love us.

So now, I think before I say I am too busy. I think about what is important. I think about how Jesus would handle the situation and what he would tell someone if they needed help. I do not always live up to these high standards of Jesus, but I do take the time to think about what is important, even if I fail to acknowledge that importance. Luckily, I can always try again. I can always try again to love.

Week 3-Tuesday

Is life what you make it?

[1] Be careful to follow every command I am giving you today, so that you may live and increase and may enter and possess the land that the LORD promised on oath to your forefathers. [2] Remember how the LORD your God led you all the way in the desert these forty years, to humble you and to test you in order to know what was in your heart, whether or not you would keep his commands. [3] He humbled you, causing you to hunger and then feeding you with manna, which neither you nor your fathers had known, to teach you that man does not live on bread alone but on every word that comes from the mouth of the LORD. [4] Your clothes did not wear out and your feet did not swell during these forty years. (Deuteronomy 8:1-4)

There are times that we have very little control of what happens to us. We may start out with a plan for the day and soon we find that life twists us and turns us in a different direction. However, is it important what that direction is, or is it more important how we travel down the road? If we look at our life as a part of God's plan, it should not surprise us when what we plan, is somehow changed. We may not be able travel down our chosen road, but we can travel through the unknown road with faith and trust in God and in his plan for us. We may not know where we are going, but we know that we will have the constant companionship with a God who loves us and wants us to live our life with joy. We may not know what it is that makes us happy or brings us joy. However, we can be certain that if we follow God's plan for our lives, we will experience joy and peace.

We can control our ability to be flexible and let our life unfold, as God wants it to. We can control our ability to sit quietly and let God speak to us and then to him. We can also go kicking and screaming, demanding that we must follow our own plan. We have the freedom to do that, but I do not believe that we will find true happiness relying upon our own efforts to make a joyful life.

I examine my life daily to determine when I experience that joy of life. It is usually when I let go of my own stubborn plan and let God work his magic in my life. So if things don't seem to be going the way you want them to go, stop and sit with God and listen to that small voice, and let God lead you in his direction. I guarantee that you will not be disappointed.

Week 3-Wednesday

So, what is the Soul?

34Then he called the crowd to him along with his disciples and said: "If anyone would come after me, he must deny himself and take up his cross and follow me. 35For whoever wants to save his life[a] will lose it, but whoever loses his life for me and for the gospel will save it. 36What good is it for a man to gain the whole world, yet forfeit his soul? 37Or what can a man give in exchange for his soul? 38If anyone is ashamed of me and my words in this adulterous and sinful generation, the Son of Man will be ashamed of him when he comes in his Father's glory with the holy angels." (Mark 8:34-38)

To progress along our individual paths of spirituality it is necessary to develop an understanding of the soul. Our soul is not something that we have; it is something that we are. The soul is the life energy within a human person. The soul is what gives life. It is also the adhesive that holds us together, the principle of integration and individuation within us. As long as we are alive, which means that we have a soul within us, all of the chemicals within us work together to form a body. At the point of death, we no longer have a body. Chemicals that used to work together begin to go their own way. Once the soul has left the body, decomposition occurs. Life stops and we literally fall apart.

The soul has a dual purpose. It puts the fire in our veins and keeps us energized, vibrant, living with zest and a sense of hope. It also keeps us fixed together. It gives us a sense of who we are, where we came from and where we are going. We are given this gift of fire, our souls become illuminated, and we are invited to live in the presence of God.

Faith in Jesus Christ enriches the soul because the message of Jesus is all about love, hope, and belonging. To feed the soul within us, we are all given the invitation to experience God's love and life. God has already accepted us as his beloved children, it is now up to us to understand and accept God's invitation to be loved. God is all you need.

Week 3-Thursday

Life's Spiritual Journey and the Labyrinth.

"Your life is a sacred journey. In addition, it is about change, growth, discovery, movement, transformation, continuously expanding your vision of what is possible, stretching your soul, learning to see clearly and deeply, listening to your intuition, taking courageous challenges at every step along the way. You are on the path...exactly where you are meant to be right now...And from here, you can only go forward, shaping your life story into a magnificent tale of triumph, of healing of courage, of beauty, of wisdom, of power, of dignity, and of love."

Caroline Adams

This is a Labyrinth

We are all on the path...exactly where we need to be. The labyrinth is a model of that path.

A labyrinth is an ancient symbol that relates to wholeness. It combines the imagery of the circle and the spiral into a meandering but purposeful path. The Labyrinth represents a journey to our own center and back again out into the world. Labyrinths have long been used as meditation and prayer tools.

A labyrinth is an archetype with which we can have a direct experience. We can walk it. It is a metaphor for life's journey. It is a symbol that creates a sacred space and place and takes us out of our ego to "That Which Is Within."

Labyrinths and mazes have often been confused. When most people hear of a labyrinth, they think of a maze. A labyrinth is not a maze. A maze is like a puzzle to be solved. It has twists, turns, and blind alleys. It is a left-brain task that requires logical, sequential, analytical activity to find the correct path into the maze and then out of the maze.

A labyrinth has only one path. It is universal. The way in is the way out. There are no blind alleys. The path leads you on a circuitous path to the center and out again. A labyrinth is a right brain task. It involves intuition, creativity, and imagery. With a maze, many choices must be made and an active mind is needed to solve the problem of finding the center. With a labyrinth, there is only one choice to be made. The choice is to enter or not. A more passive, receptive mindset is needed. The choice is whether to walk a spiritual path.

At its most basic level the labyrinth is a metaphor for the journey to the center of your deepest self and back out into the world with a broadened understanding of whom you are. Labyrinths can be walked in many ways. Different images and metaphors can be used as an aid to the experience. In this section, I want to give examples of brief rituals that can enliven the labyrinth experience. A ritual is a structured experience designed to celebrate life. It creates a container in which we can learn more about ourselves and our relationships with others. A ritual deepens our connection to our psychological and spiritual center.

Labyrinth is an interactive installation for spiritual journeys. It is for anyone who wants a break from surfing the surface of culture to contemplate the deeper things of life. Labyrinth reshapes a 12th-century ritual for the 21st century. It takes you on a symbolic journey, creates space to unwind and think—in particular about our relationships with one another, planet, our God, and ourselves.

The path has three stages—the 'inward' journey, the centre, and the 'outward' journey. The theme of the 'inward' journey is letting go of things, which hinder our wholeness and inner approach to God. The centre of the Labyrinth is a space of meditative prayer and peace. The theme of the 'outward' journey is relationship—with ourselves, with others and with the planet—seen in the light of our relationship with God.

Find a Labyrinth near you and try out this ritual for yourself.

Week 3-Friday

Our Christian Responsibility to Love is not so bad!

"So we, who are many, are one body in Christ, and individually we are members one of another." (Romans 12:5)

As St. Paul writes in his following letter to the Corinthians, love must be the focus of our lives.

"And I will show you a still more excellent way. If I speak in the tongues of men and of angels, but have not love, I am a noisy gong or a clanging cymbal. And if I have prophetic powers, and understand all mysteries and all knowledge, and if I have all faith, so as to remove mountains, but have not love, I am nothing. If I give away all I have, and if I deliver my body to be burned, but have not love, I gain nothing. Love is patient and kind, love is not jealous or boastful; it is not arrogant or rude. Love does not insist on its own way; it is not irritable or resentful; it does not rejoice at wrong, but rejoices in the right. Love bears all things, believes all things, hopes all things, and endures all things. Love never ends. As for prophecy, it will pass away; as for tongues, they will cease; as for knowledge, it will pass away. For our knowledge is imperfect and our prophecy is imperfect; but when the perfect comes, the imperfect will pass away. When I was a child, I spoke like a child; I thought like a child, I reasoned like a child. When I became a man, I gave up childish ways. For now, we see in a mirror dimly, but then face to face. Now I know in part; then I shall understand fully, even as I have been fully understood. So faith, hope, love abide, these three; but the greatest of these is love. Make love your aim, and earnestly desire the spiritual gifts." (1 Cor. 13-14:1)

The ending statement from St. Paul references the spiritual gifts. The proper use of our spiritual gifts must be guided by a constant focus on love. Each of us possesses our own spiritual gifts given to us by God. We are given different gifts to encourage us to come together and help each other in our community. We must take a risk and love each other because only in loving one another can we truly love God.

When we choose to bring unconditional love into our personal, professional, community and family lives, we begin to restore wholeness and happiness to our world. We recognize the "Kingdom is at hand." The effort to love as Jesus loves us is rewarded in the realization that we have gained a new perspective on everything and every part of our lives and the lives of the people we touch are benefited.

"And this is his commandment that we believe in the name of his Son Jesus Christ and love one another, just as he has commanded us. Whoever keeps his commandments abides in God and God in him. And by this we know that he abides in us, by the Spirit whom he has given us." (1 John 3:23-24)

Choosing Jesus

"I am the Way—yes, and the Truth and the Life. No one can get to the Father except by means of me." (John 14:6)

Jesus in not presenting an obstacle, rather, he presents an invitation to share life with him.

Even though Jesus chooses us first, we still need to choose to follow Him in our everyday lives. Since our lifestyles reveal our inner self, to connect with Jesus spiritually we must change our lifestyles, attitudes, and actions to mirror those of Jesus. We must take on the heart and mind of Jesus in everything we do and say.

Today and every day, I make the effort to love. Remember that love is a choice, not just an emotional response. To love is to care, have respect, show forgiveness, reserve judgment, and to walk with a compassionate frame of mind in all things. It is not easy, but it is very freeing to love. Loving allows people to be who they are. Loving allows you to be who you are. To love is to let go of control. Loving places you within God's Kingdom. Try love, you may be surprised that in loving

God and loving others, you will gain so much more than you give. Love will show you how to live life with "joy."

I have heard it said that, quote, "there must be a heaven, because this life is sure hell." Apparently, these people have not really understood the message of Jesus. The Kingdom is here, the Kingdom is now, and the Kingdom is love. Come join the Kingdom. Let go and love.

Week 3-Saturday

What do you think God wants you to do with your life?

As Jesus was walking beside the Sea of Galilee, he saw two brothers; Simon called Peter and his brother Andrew. They were casting a net into the lake, for they were fishermen. "Come, follow me," Jesus said, "and I will make you fishers of men." At once, they left their nets and followed him. Going on from there, he saw two other brothers, James son of Zebedee and his brother John. They were in a boat with their father Zebedee, preparing their nets. Jesus called them,2and immediately they left the boat and their father and followed him.(Matthew 4:18-22)

It is not likely that Jesus is going to call us as directly and dramatically as he called Peter and Andrew, James and John, saying face to face: "Come, follow me." However, God does call us. God knows us best. He created us, and gifted us with a unique soul and unique personality. There never was and never will be anyone quite like you or me. Just as we have unique fingerprints, we have also a unique soul. What does God want you to do with your life?

Each baptized Christian has two vocations: a general and specific vocation. Our general vocation consists in having Christ live in us and through us. We are called Christian. Even if a complete stranger meets us, that person should be able to identify us by our dress, manners, words, and deeds as a Christian. When a stranger enters your home, are there things that indicate that this is a Christian home? Is there a Bible on a table? Is there a picture of Jesus?

By appearance, are you a Christian by wearing a cross? By your words, are you Christian: praising God, not using God's name in vain? By your deeds, are you Christian by doing good and avoiding evil, by making sacrifices to do good things for other people, in imitation of Jesus?

When you do good things and help people, do you feel so good deep down that you can do this every day of your life. All people young and old ask the question: "God what do you want me to do with my life?

After you ask the question, pray quietly, and frequently. Watch and listen. What do other people say to you? Do they compliment you on sharing, on helping, on sacrificing, on your level of responsibility? If they do, excellent, give thanks to God. If people do not say these things to you, why not? If someone likes you, that is excellent; that is how God made us. More importantly, why do they like you? Is it because you have lots of money; or because you treat people well, you listen, you help, you are mature in loving God and other people…

Most importantly, ask God quietly and frequently, "God, what do you want me to do with my life?" God knows you best. He created you, uniquely. It is not likely that Jesus is going to walk up to you like the four apostles and say directly, "Come, follow me." Instead, God will guide you through prayer and experiences. Pray quietly, pray often, "God, what do you want me to do with my life?"

What do you think God wants you to do?

Are you already doing it? If so, how do you know? If not, how are you going to do it?

Take quiet time to listen to God. Since we cannot expect him to come up to us, tap us on the shoulder, and give us the directions of the day, we must sit and rest in God in quiet. Talk to God, and then listen to what he wants to say to you. A thought may come to you; a message may come from a Scripture passage or from a prayer that you speak. What God wants of you will not be complicated, and will not require a great deal of education. Whatever God wants you to do; he will give you the strength and talent to do it. Just ask him!

Week 3-Sunday

How do we connect with God?

Welcome this new day. Stretch your arms toward the sky, inhaling deeply your hopes for this day, exhaling whatever anxieties you wish to put aside.

Breathe in welcome.

Breathe out suspicion.

Repeat this several times.

Prayerfully ponder and review the distractions or obstacles that may be blocking you from receiving fully the blessings of this day.

Pass these over to God's loving care.

Sit for a few minutes in silence and offer a prayer asking for God's blessing on you during this day.

A PRAYER FOR LOVE

Teach me to love, Lord, as you love,
Make it unconditional, honest, and kind,
to ask nothing back in return, Lord,
to encompass the whole of humankind.
May I offer my love without speaking,
May it radiate as it shines forth from me,
May it be seen in my face and my eyes, Lord,
May it be simple, sincere, and shame free.
Show me how to forgive, Lord, as You do,
To not burden another with guilt,
To not play the role of the martyr,
To be a rock on which trust may be built.
Make my love for others be greater by far

than any love that is offered to me,
Led by the Spirit, Inspired of God,
As forgiving as Jesus…and free.

"*Eternal Father, I offer you the Body and Blood, Soul and Divinity of Your dearly beloved Son, Our Lord Jesus Christ, in atonement for our sins and those of the whole world.*" (Chaplet of the Divine Mercy)

Choosing is part of our everyday life. We choose all day from morning until we sleep in the evening. As children of God with free choice, we may also choose our method of attaining spirituality. Choice lies in the heart of this matter, for the spirituality chosen, if one is indeed chosen at all, will be present in the minds and attitudes of those who do the choosing. In this case, choice can influence one's entire life.

Choice, specifically concerning a rule of spirituality, is the choice of a specific set of beliefs in how to connect with Jesus. Those who authentically enter into a rule of spirituality do so by choosing these methods over all others. However, the concept of choice itself and its overall effect on a person's life varies by spirituality. Every rule of spirituality manifests this choice in different ways. Of course, choosing Jesus is the focal point. Ultimately at the heart of the choice are the person and Jesus. Underneath the entire choice of externals, one must choose whether to enter into relationship with Jesus. In choosing Jesus, one does not surrender but instead is made complete.

Remember, spirituality is not an end in itself; it is a means to find a way to walk in the presence of Jesus, to connect with Him as a friend. It is a way to follow the message of Jesus and that message is love. In order really connect with Jesus, a prayer life is extremely important. However, closing ourselves in a dark room and praying on our knees from morning to night is not necessarily the way we are called to pray. Our life has to be a prayer. We must recognize Him in everyone we meet during the course of our day. We must recognize Him in ourselves. We must live in such a way that we not only speak to Jesus, but also are able to recognize His response to us. We must love as He loves.

Week 4-Monday

What does Jesus look like?

[26]You are all children of God through faith in Christ Jesus, [27]for all of you who were baptized into Christ have clothed yourselves with Christ. [28]There is neither Jew nor Greek, slave nor free, male nor female, for you are all one in Christ Jesus. [29]If you belong to Christ, then you are Abraham's seed, and heirs according to the promise. (Galatians 3:26-20)

So, what does Jesus look like? Although even though from the Scriptures we know that he walked the earth as a man, we do not have a picture of what he looked like. Most of the pictures I have seen depict him as a white male with long brown hair and blue eyes. He was probably not white, did not have very long hair, and did not have blue eyes. In the part of the world he lived in, people did not look like that.

What he looked like was really not important. Who he was and how he treated people was what has stayed with us for over two thousand years. Being that he is God, he can look anyway he wants to. We cannot limit Jesus to a specific image.

In today's world, he could be black man, an Indian, an Anglo, or (should I say it) he could look like a woman. If Jesus is truly in all of us, he can very easily look like one of us. Jesus is in all of the people we encounter on a daily basis, both male and female, and in every color of this beautiful world, we live in. That is why we can say that the "Kingdom of God is at hand." We are Jesus, we are the kingdom. We just have not figured that out yet.

Many things happen to us as we live in the world. These things may color our perception of who we are and how we relate to other people and the world. Sometimes these things are not good, we lose sight of our significance, our talents, our need for one another, and we forget that Jesus is right there with us and in us. We may not see Jesus with us, but he is there. He is in that person who offers us a kind word when we are down. He is in the person who puts their arm around us and comforts us when we need it. He is in all of the people in whom we share both good times and bad times. He is in us, as we are there to love others.

Therefore, what does Jesus look like? Does it really matter? I think it matters more what he does within us. Looks are temporary, we all change. Just look at your baby pictures as compared to how you look now. What does not change is that we are Jesus to one another. That may seem like a big responsibility, but it really is what we are called to do and to be.

So, what does Jesus look like? He looks like you and me, “for we have clothed ourselves in Christ”.

Week 4-Tuesday

What is Prayer?

[15]*For this reason, ever since I heard about your faith in the Lord Jesus and your love for all the saints,* [16]*I have not stopped giving thanks for you, remembering you in my prayers.* [17]*I keep asking that the God of our Lord Jesus Christ, the glorious Father, may give you the Spirit of wisdom and revelation, so that you may know him better.* [18]*I pray also that the eyes of your heart may be enlightened in order that you may know the hope to which he has called you, the riches of his glorious inheritance in the saints,* [19]*and his incomparably great power for us who believe. That power is like the working of his mighty strength,* [20]*which he exerted in Christ when he raised him from the dead and seated him at his right hand in the heavenly realms,* [21]*far above all rule and authority, power and dominion, and every title that can be given, not only in the present age but also in the one to come.* [22]*And God placed all things under his feet and appointed him to be head over everything for the church,* [23]*which is his body, the fullness of him who fills everything in every way.* (Ephesians 1:15-23)

Paul understood the importance of prayer and tried to share that understanding with those he cared for. He prayed continually for his Christian family located in the various cities he visited. For us to understand the meaning of prayer, we must first believe that God exists, and that he is a personal being, a person who can be addressed and who responds. We must believe that God knows us, cares for us, and loves us, even more than we love ourselves. Some describe prayer as talking and listening with God. Others may call prayer love letters to God. Since prayer engages and expresses our relationship with God, the essence of prayer is communication.

Prayer is a communion of the human with the divine. We talk to God, our creator and we connect with him as father, mother, friend, lover, and savior. Whether our prayer comes from love, gratitude, and inspiration, or from fear, despair, and desperation, we talk heart-to-heart with God. When we pray we use the voice of the human, but we align with the voice of our hearts and our souls. Prayer fulfills the need humans have for God, for inspiration, for affirmation of our own souls. We talk to the one who loves and accepts us as we are.

We must feel that God has called us into a relationship with himself. Relationships require communication. Prayer is communication between a holy God and a beloved you and me. God wants to be in relationship with us and he knows we need what he can give. Through prayer, we experience life-transforming, life-renewing intimacy with the Creator of the universe.

Through prayer, we learn more and more about God's character, and how his perfect will is working itself out in our lives. Deepening our understanding of God also deepens our faith and desire to worship. As we become increasingly aware of our limitations, we can rest in the knowledge that our God is omniscient. Availing ourselves of God's counsel is a blessing of prayer.

Prayer opens our heart and mind to God, and makes us capable of receiving heavenly blessings and bringing forth fruits of virtues and perfection. Prayer attracts into our hearts the grace of the Holy Spirit, thus strengthening our faith, hope, and love. It illuminates our minds, directs our will to do good, consoles the heart in sorrow and suffering, and, in general, gives us everything that serves our true welfare.

There are different forms of prayer. The purpose of the various prayer types is for each individual to be able to find a way to experience God in their lives and to discover God's intimate will for their lives. We experience events in our lives differently according to our personality and the environment in which we were raised. Therefore, it is important to find a prayer type that is comfortable, meaningful and suits our individual personas.

The way that persons in love deepen their bond of charity with each other is through the sharing of their interior lives in an authentic and generous exchange of words, gestures, and feelings. The conversation of prayer deepens our intimacy with God by drawing us into the communication with him that leads to ultimate communion. In the process, prayer conforms us to the Lord we love so that, our will becomes united in some way with the will of God.

Have a conversation with God today. Keep in mind that conversation works both ways. Talk to God, but also listen to what God wants to say to you. Stop your busy lives for a little while and spend time with God. The only way we can develop our human relationships is with contact and conversation. Our relationship with God requires the same time and ingredients. Just as a loving friend or family member wants to hear from you and talk to you, so it is with God.

Week 4-Wednesday

Learning to Pray Earnestly

13Is any one of you in trouble? He should pray. Is anyone happy? Let him sing songs of praise. 14Is any one of you sick? He should call the elders of the church to pray over him and anoint him with oil in the name of the Lord. 15And the prayer offered in faith will make the sick person well; the Lord will raise him up. If he has sinned, he will be forgiven. 16Therefore confess your sins to each other and pray for each other so that you may be healed. The prayer of a righteous man is powerful and effective.

17Elijah was a man just like us. He prayed earnestly that it would not rain, and it did not rain on the land for three and a half years. 18Again he prayed, and the heavens gave rain, and the earth produced its crops. 19My brothers, if one of you should wander from the truth and someone should bring him back, 20remember this: Whoever turns a sinner from the error of his way will save him from death and cover over a multitude of sins. (James 5:13-20)

What does it mean to "learn to pray earnestly"?

In this kind of prayer you have to involve your emotions and literally catapult yourself into your prayer. It's not a casual exercise but a serious-minded endeavor, intense, with a singleness of purpose, such that you aren't distracted by anything that's unrelated to your goal. Learning to pray earnestly means that during this kind of prayer you have to turn off all distractions so that you can pray effectively.

This was the kind of prayer Elijah prayed when he prayed that it should not rain on the earth for three and a half years (James 5:17). 1 Kings 18 throws more light on how he prayed earnestly: "And Elijah went up to the top of Carmel; and he cast himself down upon the earth, and put his face between his knees" (1 Kings 18:42). Elijah put off every distraction and that is why he got such great results.

So if ever you are encountered with a difficult situation, learn to pray earnestly. Look for a quiet place where you can shut yourself away from all distractions and focus all your energies on the Lord. You have to learn to pray earnestly and refuse to allow your mind to daydream.

Cast your entire self and emotions into that prayer, for the earnest, heartfelt prayer of a sincere petitioner produces results; it makes tremendous power available, dynamic in its working. The results your want are based on your ability in learning to pray earnestly. Earnestly pray for the Lord's help in everything you do and never try to do anything for the Kingdom of Heaven without the Lord's help.

Week 4-Thursday

What is Spiritual Direction?

[13]*Is any one of you in trouble? He should pray. Is anyone happy? Let him sing songs of praise.* [14]*Is any one of you sick? He should call the elders of the church to pray over him and anoint him with oil in the name of the Lord.* [15]*And the prayer offered in faith will make the sick person well; the Lord will raise him up. If he has sinned, he will be forgiven.* [16]*Therefore confess your sins to each other and pray for each other so that you may be healed. The prayer of a righteous man is powerful and effective." (James 5:13-16)*

In the first century, the early Christians supported and ministered to one another. They helped each other in the development of their spirituality. Today with all of the distractions of our hectic lifestyle, it becomes more difficult to focus on our spirituality. In recent years, a great need has arisen among Christians of all denominations to develop and foster their relationship with God. The practice of spiritual direction is centered on and concerned with a person's experiences of his or her relationship with God.

Spiritual direction is the help given by one Christian to another which enables one to be able to understand how God is communicating with them and how they should communicate with God. The spiritual director is a companion accompanying one on their spiritual journey. We all need a way to cope with these troubling and unsettling times. The search for the rock upon which we can ground our search for meaning is not found in the things of the world. The rock is God and spiritual direction can become our roadmap on the journey to find God in our lives.

The present day practice of spiritual direction is not only encouraged for the religious, but is also encouraged for the spirituality of the laity. Spiritual direction is a relationship in which one person assists another, in attending to God's presence and call. Spiritual direction has been, and remains, particularly strong within Roman Catholic and Orthodox religious orders, and over the past twenty years

Anglican and Protestant traditions have begun to recover it more fully. There is also growing interest in spiritual direction among other faith traditions, such as Judaism and Buddhism.

We define Christian spiritual direction as help given by one Christian to another which enables that person to pay attention to God's personal communication to him or her, to respond to this personally communicating God, to grow in intimacy with this God, and to live out the consequences of the relationship. Throughout Christian history, spiritual direction has traditionally been practiced by ordained clergy alone. In recent years, however, this practice has widened to embrace the spiritual gifts of non-ordained persons as well. Today, spiritual direction is regarded as a ministry open to all, not an order or office reserved for the few.

Do you need help with your relationship with God? Would you like to develop a better prayer life? Do you see God's work in your life? Maybe Spiritual Direction could help you.

Week 4-Friday

A Prayer of Love

"Love is patient, love is kind. It does not envy, it does not boast, it is not proud. It is not rude, it is not self-seeking, it is not easily angered, it keeps no record of wrongs. Love does not delight in evil but rejoices with the truth. It always protects, always trusts, always hopes, and always perseveres." 1 Corinthians 13:4-7

Dear Lord:

Because love is patient:

Help me to be slow to judge, but quick to listen, hesitant to criticize, but eager to encourage, remembering your endless patience with me.

Because love is kind:

Help my words to be gentle and my actions to be thoughtful. Remind me to smile and to say "Please" and "Thank You" because those little things still mean so much.

Because love does not envy or boast, and it is not proud:

Help me have a heart that is humble and sees the good in others. May I celebrate and appreciate all that I have and all that I am, as well as doing the same for those around me.

Because love is not rude or self-seeking:

Help me to speak words that are easy on the ear and on the heart. When I am tempted to be wrapped up in my own little world, remind me there is a great big world out there full of needs and hurts.

Because love is not easily angered and keeps no record of wrongs:

Help me to forgive others as you have forgiven me. When I want to hold onto a grudge, gently help me release it so I can reach out with a hand of love instead.

Because love does not delight in evil but rejoices with the truth:

Help me stand up for what is right and good. May I defend the defenseless, and help the helpless. Show me how I can make a difference.

Because love always protects and always trusts:

Help me to be a refuge for those around me. When the world outside is harsh and cold, may my heart be a place of acceptance and warmth.

Finally, because love always perseveres:

Help my heart continually beat with love for you and others. AMEN.

Week 4-Saturday

Neither Jew nor Greek, neither slave nor free neither male or female?

"There is neither Jew nor Greek, there is neither slave nor free person, there is not male and female; for you are all one in Christ Jesus." (Galatians 3:28)

Is that correct? Are we all one in Christ Jesus? Did Jesus distinguish the male soul from the female soul? The Roman Church has gotten the message for two out of those three stipulations. They seem to understand the neither Jew nor Greek part (we are all welcome no matter what race or nationality); they seem to understand the neither slave nor free part (we are all equal in God's eyes); but they cannot seem to grasp the neither male nor female part.

Jesus set an example for His church, he taught both women and men. Many of these women were mentioned by name in the Gospels. At times, this value Jesus gave to women as disciples embarrassed his male followers. Once, when Jesus was found talking to a woman of Samaria about her faith, his male disciples *"watched in guarded silence"* (John 4:1-26). They marveled that he was speaking with a woman about her faith.

In Paul's letters, he acknowledged the value of women leaders within the churches. Some years after leaving Philippi, he wrote to the congregation there, entreating two women leaders, Euodia and Syntyche, to end a dispute between them the fact that he named these women indicates their importance within the church. Paul took it for granted that within Christianity, women as well as men could receive the same gifts, offer the same services, and perform the same activities.

Women exercised the gift of prophecy in the age of Paul. Besides Paul himself, seven men and four women are identified as prophets in the Book of Acts. Paul referred to the act of women praying and prophesying during public worship, and he did so in a casual manner, as if the practice were well established.

The advent of Jesus Christ means that we can no longer regard anyone from just a human point of view. We are more than our outward appearance. Does God love women in a different way than he loves men? According to St. Paul, unless the Roman church is going to drop that last stipulation (not male or female) from this text of the letter of Paul, they need to search for a better understanding of its meaning.

Week 4-Sunday

Jesus continues to encourage us to love.

"Love your enemies, bless them that curse you, do good to them that hate you, and pray for them which despitefully use you, and persecute you" (Matthew 5:44).

Jesus dealt with many aspects of human life but the one that He spent longest on was the need for love. His focus was not just on the love for our friends and family, but something much more challenging, a love that tests every normal human reaction.

He spoke of a love for those who we want to hate, a love for those who already hate us. This love requires effort, and strain, and every ounce of self-command that one can summon up. It is the easiest thing in the world to hate, to let the desire for revenge grow in our hearts. Indeed vengeance may even have the shadow of justice attached to it, but in reality, it leads to dark, unadulterated hate and a spiral of destruction.

To be truly happy we must rise above the bigotry and jealousy of others. We must love even if we are hated for it. Love and do not hate, for surely love is the only path to peace, freedom, and happiness. Those who follow the path of love will be demonstrating the kingdom of heaven that Jesus was trying to tell us about. God's Kingdom is at hand.

Week 5-Monday

Love Your Enemies?

[43]"You have heard that it was said, 'Love your neighbor and hate your enemy.' [44]But I tell you: Love your enemies and pray for those who persecute you, [45]that you may be sons of your Father in heaven. He causes his sun to rise on the evil and the good, and sends rain on the righteous and the unrighteous. [46]If you love those who love you, what reward will you get? Are not even the tax collectors doing that? [47]And if you greet only your brothers, what are you doing more than others? Do not even pagans do that? [48]Be perfect, therefore, as your heavenly Father is perfect. (Matthew 5:43-48)

This past Week, I was tested on my ability to be loving, compassionate, and forgiving. I would like to say that I passed the test, but I did not. Being a follower of Jesus, we have the responsibility to love our enemies, to forgive those who do wrong to us. This past Week, I found that to be easier said than done. I was put in a situation where I had to show love to someone I felt was difficult to deal with. I did not do this. The only thing that I can say in my defense is that I realize that I did not do this. I realize that this was a lesson that I had to learn through experience. It is easy to love those who love us. Jesus said to "love your enemies," and I thought I understood the message. However, when it was time to put these words into actions, I missed the mark.

I am grateful for the lesson. It gave me the opportunity to realize that in order to do this, I must ask for God's help. It is not something that I can accomplish on my own. It is an important realization that in the past, I might not have recognized. It may make it a little easier to remember to seek God's help when faced with difficult people.

It is arrogant to believe that we can live as followers of Christ without always seeking his help when faced with situations that may cause us to be unloving. We cannot follow him without recognizing that he is leading the way. That may not make sense, but think about it. When we try to rely on ourselves to get through difficult situations, we often fail. If we keep our eyes on Jesus and call upon his assistance to help us when we are tested, success can be ours.

Week 5-Tuesday

The Cost of Following Jesus

57As they were walking along the road, a man said to him, "I will follow you wherever you go."

58Jesus replied, "Foxes have holes and birds of the air have nests, but the Son of Man has no place to lay his head." 59He said to another man, "Follow me." But the man replied, "Lord, first let me go and bury my father." 60Jesus said to him, "Let the dead bury their own dead, but you go and proclaim the kingdom of God." 61Still another said, "I will follow you, Lord; but first let me go back and say good-by to my family." 62Jesus replied, "No one who puts his hand to the plow and looks back is fit for service in the kingdom of God." (Matthew 8:57-62)

Why do only a few people follow Christ for a lifetime? Why do some appear to follow for a time and then fall away? What prevents us from following Jesus wholeheartedly? Why do many of us prefer to build on the sand rather than the rock?

It can't be that we don't know about Him. With all the technology available today, the archaeological research confirming the people and places of the Scriptures, the immense volumes of writings of believers explaining their faith, and the exegetical study of the words of the Bible—it's as if we know so much, yet believe so little.

It is not a matter of lack of evidence to convince people that the Scriptures is true; the problem is that they do not want to believe the Scriptures. The reason for this is obvious. If people believed in the God of the Bible, they would have no choice but to acknowledge his authority and obey the rules he has laid down.

Discipleship is a very demanding thing and the blood of the martyrs is the seed of the church. When Jesus said we should be prepared to give up our possessions, he was calling his disciples to recognize that discipleship is never a cheap thing. What is more, Jesus proved it when He went to the cross in our place. The truth is, when you're following Jesus, people aren't always going to approve. Following Jesus means that he has to take first priority in our life, even if it is painful, difficult, and misunderstood. Jesus doesn't offer wealth or comfort or earthly security. He simply says, if you're coming with me you're going to be rejected by the world. Are you prepared to choose that?

However, as difficult as discipleship may seem, I can promise you that following Jesus is worth the cost. When we stand before God, we won't be answering to our critics, but rather our biggest fan and loved one who will be so pleased with what we've accomplished in the face of opposition. When we stand in God's presence, when we hear the words "well done, good and faithful servant" any price we may have paid here in this earthly world, will look silly in comparison to the rewards that await us in with Jesus in eternity.

Therefore, what does Jesus expect us to give up to follow him?
What are we willing to give up in order to follow Jesus?
What does Jesus ask all of us to do?

I think that the question really is, what we can give in exchange for so great a love as his. What will we give? For you see, two thousand years or so after he lived on earth there is still something exciting and magnetic about this Jesus of Nazareth that draws people to him. It must be the power of God behind his word, and the authority with which he calls us to serve him even now. Following Jesus is not an easy thing, but his word is still the best news this world has ever heard for bad times or good, and that is what you and I are called to remember together. Discipleship is a demanding thing. Discipleship is a delightful thing, and discipleship is a determined thing. If you would follow him, come with all you are and with all you have. Following Jesus is worth it. As Peter asked Jesus in John's Gospel, "to whom else will we go"?

Week 5-Wednesday

Prayer and Scripture

[5]"And when you pray, do not be like the hypocrites, for they love to pray standing in the synagogues and on the street corners to be seen by men. I tell you the truth, they have received their reward in full. [6]But when you pray, go into your room, close the door and pray to your Father, who is unseen. Then your Father, who sees what is done in secret, will reward you. [7]And when you pray, do not keep on babbling like pagans, for they think they will be heard because of their many words. [8]Do not be like them, for your Father knows what you need before you ask him. (Matthew 6:5-8)

Prayer and connection with God is our defense against the dictates of our sterile and material seeking civilization. Prayer and connection with God is what gives us the strength to live the good news of the Gospel. Prayer does not mean simply to pour out one's heart. It means to find the way to God and to speak with him, whether the heart is full or empty. We believe scripture is God's way of communicating with us, shaping us, and informing us.

Jesus Christ wants to pray with us and to have us pray with him, so that we may be confident and glad that God hears us. We learn to speak to God because God has spoken to us and continue to speak to us. God's speech in Jesus Christ meets us in the Holy Scriptures. There is peace in the will of God, which we can discover through prayer...Spiritual formation is the process of coming to know God and allowing God's vision and values to shape us. We participate in this process through prayer. Prayer is nothing more than coming into greater consciousness of what already dwells within us and within every person and creature.

We are invited to live with a heart that yearns for life, a heart that desires God, and a heart that delights in the voice of God. The invitation is always there even if it is difficult for us to respond. As we recognize God's tremendous love for us, we grow in our love for others. When we live out of an awareness of our union with God and others, we live a life full of gratitude. Our gratitude deepens as we develop an appreciative eye. Scripture emphasizes the importance of gratitude and shows us the way to live our thankfulness. An unconditionally positive attitude moves us toward more positive life experiences. We no longer live tied to the standards, which are tied to the "normalcy of civilization."

While efficiency and control are the great aspirations of our society, the loneliness, isolation, lack of friendship and intimacy, broken relationships, boredom, feelings of emptiness and depression, and a deep sense of uselessness fill the hearts of millions of people in our success-oriented world. The Christian leader of the future is called to be completely irrelevant and to stand in this world with nothing to offer but his or her own vulnerable self. That is the way Jesus came to reveal God's love. God loves us not because of what we do or accomplish, but because God has created and redeemed us in love and has chosen us to proclaim that love as the true source of all human life.

Week 5-Thursday

Why Pray?

[9]For this reason, since the day we heard about you, we have not stopped praying for you and asking God to fill you with the knowledge of his will through all spiritual wisdom and understanding. [10]And we pray this in order that you may live a life worthy of the Lord and may please him in every way: bearing fruit in every good work, growing in the knowledge of God, [11]being strengthened with all power according to his glorious might so that you may have great endurance and patience, and joyfully [12]giving thanks to the Father, who has qualified you to share in the inheritance of the saints in the kingdom of light. [13]For he has rescued us from the dominion of darkness and brought us into the kingdom of the Son he loves, [14]in whom we have redemption, the forgiveness of sins. (Colossians 1:9-14)

All prayer begins with a desire to have something. We pray to God to grant us our wishes, to have, to be, or to do. We pray for what we want God to give what or us we want to happen to us. Prayer may take the form of asking for good health for someone or ourselves we love. It could be that we pray for something good to happen such as obtaining a new job or something bad not to happen such as the death of a loved one. Since God is the ultimate giver, we as his children ask for our many desires to be granted to us.

As children, we seek simple things. We might ask God to make it snow so we would not have to go to school. It may be forgiveness that we are seeking and we look to God as a loving father who will pick us up when we have fallen. He is our ultimate caregiver and as the provider of all things. We come to God for all our human needs. In our simplicity, we expect God to grant all our requests and as children, we can sometimes become angry with him if our desires are not granted. Our prayers to God are simple, we talk to God, or we talk at God and expect him to grant our requests.

The emphasis of our desires in prayer must move us away from the simple childlike need to constantly receive and move us toward a real connection with the God who is with us and in us. It is in this manner that we satisfy the souls longing to feel his presence and to abide in his embrace. It is to experience his ultimate destiny for us.

When our prayer life matures, we do not always have a desire for things; we also have a desire to be a part of the world around us. Through contemplative prayer, our hearts, minds, and souls desire a deeper meaning in life. We have a desire at the level of our soul to connect with our divine creator. Prayer to God articulates our longing and desire to find his love and to experience that love within us. We want God to be with us and we want to be with God. Prayer not only becomes a talking to God, but also now we seek to listen to what God has to tell us. We pray to seek his desires for us and we desire to do his will.

Our desire in prayer now takes the form of communication with God. Just as communication is the way we get to know one another, we seek to get to know God. Our prayers of desire now involve the wish to be a part of his life and his creation. We seek a deep connection with others as well as a deep connection with God.

We learn more and more about his character and how his perfect will is working itself out in our lives. Deepening our understanding of God also deepens our faith and desire to worship. As we become increasingly aware of our limitations, we can rest in the knowledge that our God is omniscient. Availing ourselves of God's counsel is a blessing of prayer.

We do not have all the answers to the why and how of life. Isn't it comforting to know that we do not need to know all the answers? It is freeing to understand that we are not in control. To pray is to rest in God's guidance. It is to begin to let go and just be who we are.

God loves us just as we are and prayer with God helps us to find out who we are instead of trying to be something we are not.

Week 5-Friday

It is in the quiet that we hear God's voice.

1 The boy Samuel ministered before the LORD under Eli. In those
days the word of the LORD was rare; there were not many visions.

2 One night Eli, whose eyes were becoming so weak that he could
barely see, was lying down in his usual place. 3 The lamp of God had
not yet gone out, and Samuel was lying down in the temple[l] of the
LORD, where the ark of God was. 4 Then the LORD called Samuel.
Samuel answered, "Here I am." 5 And he ran to Eli and said, "Here
I am; you called me."
But Eli said, "I did not call; go back and lie down. " So he went and
lay down.

6 Again the LORD called, "Samuel! " And Samuel got up and went
to Eli and said, "Here I am; you called me."
"My son," Eli said, "I did not call; go back and lie down."

7 Now Samuel did not yet know the LORD: The word of the LORD
had not yet been revealed to him.

8 The LORD called Samuel a third time, and Samuel got up and went
to Eli and said, "Here I am; you called me."
Then Eli realized that the LORD was calling the boy. 9 So Eli told
Samuel, "Go and lie down, and if he calls you, say, 'Speak, LORD, for
your servant is listening.' " So Samuel went and lay down in his place.

10 The LORD came and stood there, calling as at the other times,
"Samuel! Samuel!"
Then Samuel said, "Speak, for your servant is listening."

In the busyness of our lives, we seldom stop to hear the voice of those who wish to speak to us. I know that when someone is trying to speak to me as I move from one task to another, I do not hear what he or she is saying. I am only concentrating on the task at hand. When I am busy, I do not even listen to my own thoughts and most of the time I do not even take the time to think at all. I am driven, focused, and blind to everything that is going on around me.

In this busyness of mine, I could not possibly be having much conversation with God. I could not have much of a conversation with anyone in my task-oriented mode. It is only when I stop my busyness, take the time to rest and listen, can I converse with God. I can hear him in my thoughts, in the stillness.

When you stop and take the time to reflect, you can see how he was present to you during your day; how he spoke to you in the people that you encountered during the day. God will not tap you on the shoulder and tell you to listen to him. God will wait patiently for you to recognize that he is there with you and waits patiently for conversation with you. I feel that God speaks to you all the time, but you cannot possibly know that unless you stop, rest, and listen.

Week 5-Saturday

We are all significant in the eyes of Jesus.

"And, oh, what a great love it is! Nothing can separate us from it. "Neither death nor life, nor angels nor principalities nor powers, nor things present nor things to come, nor height nor depth, nor any other created thing, shall be able to separate us from the love of God which is in Christ Jesus our Lord." (Romans 8:38-39)

I have always had a great love for the writings of St. Paul. He is an inspiration in that he changed his life after his encounter with Jesus on the road to Damascus and he wrote with such feeling and love for the people he converted to Christianity. In this short passage from Romans, he has shared his own spirituality and has told of God's great love for us which is unconditional and forever. It has helped me to formulate my own understanding of true spirituality and how it must be manifested in my own life.

In my quest for true spirituality, Jesus speaks to my dark side with his eternal message of love. I long for true spiritual connection with him that transcends my hurried existence and from which I can leave the world of temporary and changing and secure a sense of permanent and unchangeable. I know that I can only receive this security by developing my relationship with Jesus. Security will not come from a new age therapy, from the accumulation of wealth, nor from any of my earthly relationships. I come to Jesus, embracing my spiritual bankruptcy and brokenness, and seek His love and acceptance. I know that I cannot come to Him on my terms, but come to Him on His terms and also with His assistance.

Jesus tells me that I am significant. He tells you the same thing.

Week 5-Sunday

How heavy is the yolk on your soul?

28 "Come to me, all you who are weary and burdened, and I will give you rest. 29 Take my yoke upon you and learn from me, for I am gentle and humble in heart, and you will find rest for your souls. 30 For my yoke is easy and my burden is light." (Matthew 11:28-30)

In our day and age, no matter how high the standards of living reach or how physically comfortable we try to become; true peace of heart still does not exist. On the contrary, each individual feels some kind of fear, a deep-seated restlessness within him or herself.

These are all indications of the soul's pressure on the body, warning the person of the wrong path that he or she has chosen to follow. Hence, some kind of grievous depression or anxiety makes the person worry and feel sad, but without a clear reason. These are all signs of the soul's distress and the effect of the heart's discomfort in a person, due to his/her not paying attention to the Soul's nutritional needs, and instead focusing on strictly human material matters.

Furthermore, many of us today are deceived into thinking that more material things actually give us the strength to satisfy that cry from within us; that cry that says, "If I could just get others to like and accept me, I'd be happy…" or "If I could just get someone to say something good about me, tell me I look better, or am better than so and so…" or "If I were rich and had power or influence it would be enough…" Do you hear and allow yourself to be burdened down by that inner cry for strength? If you had all the wealth, power, position, favor, or publicity, would it ever be enough? No. In addition, neither would you possess the inner strength or real joy that your soul craves.

Even if you should become King or Queen of the entire world, without satisfying the needs of your Soul, it would not be very long before you would again be asking, "Is this all there is…?" "Is there any more?" Material things are never enough because they do not strengthen your inner being (i.e. your soul) or satisfy the craving within which causes people to reach out for possessions, fortune and fame, drugs, alcohol, self-gratification etc, all in an attempt to satisfy the Soul. The soul is something that in the end does not depend on material things.

When in an attempt to gain a level of comfort, people become excessive in any area of their life, be it excessive jewelry, clothing, purchases, habits, etc. they only receive a temporary calm to satisfy and soothe that inner cry for real joy which originates from within. The next day, the next Week, or some other time later, that cry starts over again, only this time a bit louder and a bit more urgent.

Perhaps also, we then try to throw ourselves into religion believing that this will satisfy our soul. We become involved in many activities of the particular church we attend thinking that we will find happiness and rest for our soul. This seems to be good, but it is just another part of being busy. This, too, can become just an additional burden. We again think by being busy in these good activities, we will find peace in our soul. Wrong again. We have still missed the point of the needs of the soul. We have again missed the discovery that our soul does not need things or activities to be at peace, we just need relationship with Jesus.

That relationship requires us not to be busy, but to be still and at rest and to listen. We cannot develop relationships if we do not spend time with the object of our relationship. We need to be in conversation, spending time, learning to understand this person with whom we desire a relationship. Therefore, it is with Jesus. We need to take time to rest, reflect, and pray (the way to conversation with Jesus). We must also know that we cannot have peace of soul without his assistance. We cannot do it on our own. This is the meaning of the term "rest in God." Stop your constant need to be active and take the time just to be with Jesus. His invitation is very clear to all of us.

28 "Come to me, all you who are weary and burdened, and I will give you rest. 29 Take my yoke upon you and learn from me, for I am gentle and humble in heart, and you will find rest for your souls. 30 For my yoke is easy and my burden is light." (Matthew 11:28-30)

Week 6-Monday

Accepting God's Word and living it.
We cannot give what we have not first received.

[14]How, then, can they call on the one they have not believed in? And how can they believe in the one of whom they have not heard? And how can they hear without someone preaching to them? [15]And how can they preach unless they are sent? As it is written, "How beautiful are the feet of those who bring good news!"

[16]But not all the Israelites accepted the good news. For Isaiah says, "Lord, who has believed our message?" [17]Consequently, faith comes from hearing the message, and the message is heard through the word of Christ. (Romans 10:14-17)

Each of us is called to a personal relationship with a God who loves us. Each of us needs to listen to God's Word as it is written in the Scriptures. Each of us, by the power of the Holy Spirit, must make a decision to surrender to God's love and to commit ourselves to follow Christ. Each of us needs the support of a faith community to experience God's love and empower us to go out to others.

Living It Out: Our lives speak more clearly than our words.

"Do not deceive yourselves by just listening to God's Word; instead, put it into practice ... For whoever looks closely into the perfect law that sets people free, who keeps on paying attention to it and does not simply listen and then forget it, but puts it into practice, that person will be blessed by God is what is done." (James 1:22-25)

Each of us is called to share the love we have received with others. Each of us can show care for each person we meet at work, on the street, and in times of leisure. Each of us who is a member of a family can express our love for each other within the family. As a family, we can show love toward others. Each faith community must let people know that they are Disciples of Christ by the love they have for one another. Each of us is called to help others as effectively as we can especially the poor and the marginalized.

Listen to God's word today and share it with someone you love.

Week 6-Tuesday

This Life Goes by Quickly

[17]Some of his disciples said to one another, "What does he mean by
saying, 'In a little while you will see me no more, and then after a little
while you will see me,' and 'Because I am going to the Father'?"
[18]They kept asking, "What does he mean by 'a little while'? We don't
understand what he is saying."
[19]Jesus saw that they wanted to ask him about this, so he said to
them, "Are you asking one another what I meant when I said, 'In a little
while you will see me no more, and then after a little while you will see
me'? [20]I tell you the truth, you will weep and mourn while the world
rejoices. You will grieve, but your grief will turn to joy. [21]A woman
giving birth to a child has pain because her time has come; but when
her baby is born she forgets the anguish because of her joy that a child
is born into the world. [22]So with you: Now is your time of grief, but I will
see you again and you will rejoice, and no one will take away your joy.
[23]In that day you will no longer ask me anything. I tell you the truth, my
Father will give you whatever you ask in my name. [24]Until now you
have not asked for anything in my name. Ask and you will receive, and
your joy will be complete. (John 16:17-24)

Our life passes so quickly and before you know it, life can pass you by without your even realizing that you have missed what is important. We spend a lot of time planning for the future. We accumulate things and try to save money so that we will be comfortable in our later years. However, before we realize it, those years are upon us and we have not fostered the one area in our life that is really important and that will satisfy our every need. We have not fostered our relationship with God.

Perhaps we have not even thought about the fact that a relationship with God is important.

All the other things we accumulate are temporary. They can be taken away at a moment's notice. Just look at how the economy went south in 2008-2009. Some people lost all savings, homes, cars, and other items of accumulation. Our security is not in what we can save and accumulate on earth, but in our relationship with the God who loves us. We can never lose that. God is always there and will not abandon us in times of trouble. When all else fails, God will still be there with us.

Even if the economy had not failed, we can save all our lives for our retirement and die before we have a chance to enjoy the fruits of our labor. If we put our efforts and trust in God, we will always enjoy the fruits of that labor. True, it is good to plan for the future, but not to be held captive to that future. We should not become slaves to what we possess.

Our hearts and minds should be attuned to our love of God and others and in that; we will find true happiness and security. Things are temporary, God is permanent. I sometimes look at the wealthy of our society to see if they are really happy with all they possess. They must protect and guard all of their wealth so others will not take it away. Even with all they have, they still do not seem happy. Some drink, take drugs, or indulge in unhealthy or unsavory activities.

Those who have found the love of God, however, seem to be happy and at peace, even though in earthly wealth, they may have very little or nothing. Their lives are spent helping and loving others.

So, as this year speeds by, thing about what makes you happy? Do all you possess of worldly goods satisfy your needs? Are you looking forward to finally having enough earthly wealth and realizing that there is never enough? Do you treasure the earthly relationships in your life, as well as your relationship with God? Do you work to preserve those relationships? I ask myself what do I want to accomplish. I ask myself what is important to me. What do I want to pursue? It is the accumulation of wealth, or the accumulation of love.

Therefore, think about what is important to you. What do you want? What makes you happy? What is satisfying about your life? Each new day, new month, New Year, gives us new beginnings. What do you want in your new beginnings? Is God in the plan for your new beginning? How about your relationships with others? Something to think about.

Week 6-Wednesday

A Ministry of Reconciliation

*[11]Since, then, we know what it is to fear the Lord, we try to persuade
men. What we are is plain to God, and I hope it is also plain to your
conscience. [12]We are not trying to commend ourselves to you again, but
are giving you an opportunity to take pride in us, so that you can
answer those who take pride in what is seen rather than in what is in the
heart. [13]If we are out of our mind, it is for the sake of God; if we are in
our right mind, it is for you. [14]For Christ's love compels us, because we
are convinced that one died for all, and therefore all died. [15]And he died
for all, that those who live should no longer live for themselves but for
him who died for them and was raised again.*

*[16]So from now on we regard no one from a worldly point of view.
Though we once regarded Christ in this way, we do so no longer.
[17]Therefore, if anyone is in Christ, he is a new creation; the old has
gone, the new has come! [18]All this is from God, who reconciled us to
himself through Christ and gave us the ministry of reconciliation:
[19]that God was reconciling the world to himself in Christ, not counting
men's sins against them. And he has committed to us the message of
reconciliation. [20]We are therefore Christ's ambassadors, as though
God were making his appeal through us. We implore you on Christ's
behalf: Be reconciled to God. [21]God made him who had no sin to be sin
for us, so that in him we might become the righteousness of God. (2
Corinthians 5:11-21)*

"Forgive us our sins, as we forgive those who trespass against us." We profess these words every time we say "The Lord's Prayer." However, when we say it, do we realize what we are saying? Do we realize that we are professing to practice forgiveness and reconciliation? As ambassadors of Christ, we have the responsibility to love one another. However, how do we show this love? Do we only love those who behave as we think they should? Do we stop loving when we are hurt or disappointed?

It is my belief that no act shows greater love than that of forgiveness. This life-giving power of forgiveness stems from its nature as a whole new way of life.

Not to forgive is to allow our wounds to blind us; to forgive means to see again. We see ourselves, as we really are, no longer the helpless victim, but rather one who also has hurt others; one who is loved infinitely, and who, in Christ, has the inner capacity to love generously. To forgive is to see those who have hurt us as they really are, not as evil adversaries, but as brothers and sisters who struggle with and suffer from their own weakness and hurts and wounds. Our very will to forgive in this way opens us both, forgiver and forgiven, to a future that is loving and new. Not to forgive causes us to stay buried and bitter in a past that will only serve to cripple and destroy us. Love, as Christ teaches us, compels us to forgive and to be welcoming to those who have injured us.

We cannot truly forgive unless we also seek reconciliation. We, as the church community, should always be willing to take up the task of reconciliation among ourselves and labor to open up our hearts to one another in the spirit of love and forgiveness. . Without forgiveness, there is no reconciliation, and without reconciliation, there can be no real church community and the Kingdom of God, of which Christ spoke, does not exist.

To live our lives as a sacrament of reconciliation is, of course, beyond our own powers. We learn this hard lesson every time we look for reconciliation and meet instead what seems to be hopeless heartache. The truth is that we ourselves injure others, just as others injure us. We eventually learn by our own experience that to forgive is to also to try to forget a hurt or injury. Anyone who has tried to forgive and to become reconciled knows that our efforts are useless unless they are upheld by the grace and mercy of Jesus Christ. We cannot on our own change or open up human heart, not even our own.

However, there is one who can, and who has reconciled to God not only us, but also all of humanity, past, present and future, "making peace through the blood of his cross" (Col 1:20). It is in Christ that we can, along with our own labors, make of our life a ministry of reconciliation by constant prayer for ourselves and for those with whom we need and long to be reconciled.

As a lay minister in the Catholic Church, it is my responsibility to be an Ambassador of Christ. By my actions, I must strive to be an example to the community of Christ's teachings and His way of living. I must become a minister of reconciliation. To do this, I must make love, forgiveness, and reconciliation the cornerstones of my life. With the help of Jesus Christ, this task may become easier for me.

Week 6-Thursday

Who is Jesus?

[1] The Spirit of the Sovereign LORD is on me,
because the LORD has anointed me
to preach good news to the poor.
He has sent me to bind up the brokenhearted,
to proclaim freedom for the captives
and release from darkness for the prisoners, [a]

[2] to proclaim the year of the LORD's favor
and the day of vengeance of our God,
to comfort all who mourn,

[3] and provide for those who grieve in Zion—
to bestow on them a crown of beauty
instead of ashes,
the oil of gladness
instead of mourning,
and a garment of praise
instead of a spirit of despair.
They will be called oaks of righteousness,
a planting of the LORD
for the display of his splendor.
(Isaiah 61:1-3)

Jesus Christ is one the most fascinating figures in history. Despite his humble origins, short life, and very short public career, Jesus is the central focus of the world's largest religion and has meant many things to many people since his death over 2,000 years ago. However, who is Jesus Christ from a Catholic theological perspective?

When I was a child going to Catholic School, the Nuns taught us that Jesus Christ is true God and true man. At that time, I just accepted the phrase as another one of those things that adults say to children that makes absolutely no sense what so ever. When I asked what exactly that meant, I was told, "It is a mystery." Well, that certainly clarified things for me. As an adult, I still do not think I understand exactly what that means although now I know why I do not understand. I think that the concept of the two natures of Jesus Christ is a hard concept to grasp.

Therefore, I guess an easier question is, "What should I as a Christian believe about Jesus?" I will attempt to summarize what I feel are the four major beliefs regarding Jesus.

First, Christians believe Jesus to have been a historical human being who was born of a virgin named Mary, in the town of Bethlehem, between seven and 4 BC. The humanity of Jesus is perhaps one of the least controversial areas of Christology, but this was not always so. In the early years after Christ, some thought that Jesus' body, suffering, and death were merely appearances. He was not fully human, but only appeared to be.

Second, Christians believe Jesus is the Messiah, the "anointed one" predicted in the Jewish Scriptures. The word "Christ" comes from the Greek word for "Messiah." He is the Redeemer of the world, the Savior of all humankind and the Reconciler between God and humanity by dying for our sins. It is interesting to note that although Jesus appears to see Himself as the Messiah in the Gospels, He does not go out of his way to identify Himself as such, and those who do identify Him as the Messiah are commanded not to tell anyone about it.

Third, Christians believe that Jesus is the "Son of God." Jesus does not refer to himself as the Son of God in the Gospels, but the term is used in the writings of Paul and in the epistle to the Hebrews. The Gospel of John refers to Jesus simply as "the Son," which may have a similar meaning. Paul uses the term for both Christ and Christians. Christians become sons of God by adoption, but Jesus is the rightful Son of God by nature.

Finally, Christians believe that Jesus Christ is God. This concept seems to be stated explicitly in the New Testament especially in the writings of the Gospel of John. In addition, some important titles and functions applied to Jesus in the New Testament indicate early belief in His divinity. The statement "Jesus Christ is Lord" is found throughout the New Testament and was one of the earliest Christian confessions of faith. "Lord" had come to be almost synonymous with God in Jewish thinking by the time of Jesus. New Testament writers apply functions to Jesus that are associated only with God. Jesus is the savior of humanity; it is appropriate to call on the name of Jesus in prayer and to worship him; Jesus reveals God directly *"Anyone who has seen me has seen the Father" (John 14:9).*

What does this mean to me in my ministry? I think it is important to remember that Jesus is all of the above. There is not a choice of one over the other. It is also important to understand that Jesus became human out of love for us. He gave up His life for us as the ultimate sacrifice and the ultimate expression of love. He is our God and Savior, but He is also our brother and our friend.

In the beginning of the spiritual life, we feel as if all the desiring is on our side. However, God's longing evokes and fuels our own. God's own self initiates these longings.

If God loves us first, then the above statements make perfect sense. Our relationship with God is a mutual relationship of love. Jesus ministry to us was one of bringing us back into relationship with the God who loves us first. Think about that as you go through your day. How magnificent a gift we received from Jesus. His death on the cross was an indication of the length that God goes to let us know how much he wants to be in relationship with us. God's will for us and desire for us is not just that of an authority figure wanting subjugation from his servants. God's will for us is that of one who loves wanting the best for the object of his affection, us. This would also indicate that the desire of God is that we love him back. This for me was a startling realization.

So, who is Jesus? Jesus is the God who wants us to be in relationship with him. Jesus is the God who loves us first.

Week 6-Friday

Why are we involved in ministry?

*[13]Jesus went up on a mountainside and called to him those he wanted,
and they came to him. [14]He appointed twelve—designating them
apostles—that they might be with him and that he might send them out to
preach [15]and to have authority to drive out demons. [16]These are the twelve
he appointed: Simon (to whom he gave the name Peter [17] James son of
Zebedee and his brother John (to them he gave the name Boanerges, which
means Sons of Thunder); [18]Andrew, Philip, Bartholomew, Matthew,
Thomas, James son of Alphaeus, Thaddaeus, Simon the Zealot [19]and Judas
Iscariot, who betrayed him. (Mark 3:13-19)*

Jesus acted in all situations with compassion and love. In order to be a true Christian and follower of Jesus, we need to follow his example and treat each person with compassion and love. This is why we are in ministry and what we must keep focused on in the course of carrying out our various ministries.

Jesus may have had a mission statement, but he never wrote it down, he lived it. I do not believe he made a schedule, psychologically analyzed his chosen Apostles, nor conceptualized the importance of a hierarchical structure in his new Church. He stressed how all of us were equal in God's eyes. He told us that love is the most important commandment, both of God and of neighbor. He told us that everyone is our neighbor. He told us all to go out and spread the good news.

Spreading the good news of Jesus is why we are in ministry. Whether we are lecturing, visiting the sick, planning a fundraiser, planning a liturgy, or facilitating a bible study, the main focus is and should be spreading the "Good News of Jesus." I believe that the main point of the good news is "love." If we act with love, all other problems will take care of themselves. I do not know why we have to make it so complicated. Jesus did not come to present us with a philosophical dogma. He came to tell us how we could live simply. We must love. Ministry is about fostering love.

I feel that the most important aspects of my ministry must focus on love and teaching love in everything that I do.

If I had to develop a mission statement for Christians, it would be the following:

1. to love and serve the Lord.
2. To love my neighbor.
3. To act with compassion.
4. To be patient and forgiving.
5. To follow the example of Christ in all things.

I hope that this is a mission statement that Jesus would approve.

Week 6-Saturday

God loves us even though we sin!

[1] The LORD said to me, "Go, show your love to your wife again, though she is loved by another and is an adulteress. Love her as the LORD loves the Israelites, though they turn to other gods and love the sacred raisin cakes."

[2] So I bought her for fifteen shekels [a] of silver and about a homer and a lethek [b] of barley. [3] Then I told her, "You are to live with [c] me many days; you must not be a prostitute or be intimate with any man, and I will live with [d] you."

[4] For the Israelites will live many days without king or prince, without sacrifice or sacred stones, without ephod or idol. [5] Afterward the Israelites will return and seek the LORD their God and David their king. They will come trembling to the LORD and to his blessings in the last days.

(Hosea 3:1-4)

I was reading a book on forgiveness. The book emphasized that we must be given the grace to be sorry for our sins. Even though I do agree with that, I find that some people are far too easily sorry for every little imperfection. Yes, we need to feel sorry for our sins, but we also need to feel confident that God loves us even though we sin. God's love is unconditional. It is important in life to feel accepted and many people go through life feeling very unacceptable. They do not feel confident that they are loved even by God. This is why I think that God's love message, that was brought to us by Jesus, needs to be emphasized. We are love by God, first. What does that mean?

I will say it again. God loves us first. That does not say that God will accept us if we love him. God loves us first. For some of us, that is a very significant statement, especially if we feel that we must do something in order to be loved. God loves us first. What a tremendous gift.

I think that we must also realize that we must be filled with love, before we can give love to others. God does not expect us to give love without having already experienced love. That is why we must trust in God's love. God loves us first. God loves us as we are. We can find acceptance in the eyes of God.

God's love should be something that sustains us and gives us strength. We cannot fill others with love if we do not feel loved ourselves. Take hope in God's love to transform us into what we want to become. We can only succeed in our lives with God's help. Keep in mind that God's help is God's love. When we can open ourselves and accept God's love, we will find the strength to love and to help others.

God loves us first. God loves us as we are. Do not forget that.

Week 6-Sunday

Are you a Pharisee or a Tax Collector?

9To some who were confident of their own righteousness and looked down on everybody else, Jesus told this parable:

10"Two men went up to the temple to pray, one a Pharisee and the other a tax collector. 11The Pharisee stood up and prayed about himself: 'God, I thank you that I am not like other men—robbers, evildoers, adulterers—or even like this tax collector. 12I fast twice a Week and give a tenth of all I get.' 13"But the tax collector stood at a distance. He would not even look up to heaven, but beat his breast and said, 'God, have mercy on me, a sinner.' 14"I tell you that this man, rather than the other, went home justified before God. For everyone who exalts he will be humbled, and he who humbles himself will be exalted." (Luke 18:9-14)

In this parable, Jesus brings to light the difference between man's idea of discipleship and God's idea of discipleship. We cannot follow in the footsteps of Jesus on our own merit. We must first recognize our need for forgiveness of our own sinfulness and ask for Jesus' help and guidance.

Jesus told this parable "to some who were confident of their own righteousness and looked down on everybody else." It remains as a warning to us who trust in ourselves to be without sin and who despise others for their sinfulness. This parable reveals and teaches a lesson of great importance in order for us to realize that God knows our character and purpose when we come before Him in prayer. God knows the contents of our hearts and is not fooled by the words we may say in prayer.

The Pharisee is exposed as a self-righteous person. The Pharisee because of his ego and pride is deceived into believing that God is pleased with him. His prayer starts out like thanksgiving for what God has done, but ends up as praise for what he has done for God. Sadly, in his own eyes he believes that he is better than others are. He brags about all he does beyond what is required and that as a religious man he has done everything that is right.

In contrast, we notice that the tax collector's prayer to God is filled with humility and in repentance for sin; and he desires God's mercy. He acknowledged that he was a sinner guilty before God and that he relies and is dependent only upon the mercy and grace of God. The tax collector comes to the temple realizing that God is a holy, majestic and an all-powerful being. This is revealed in the manner the tax collector approaches; comes with timidity, from a distance, not lifting his eyes to heaven and in humility. The tax collector has no doubt that he is in need of God's assistance to do what is right. He knows that he is nothing without God.

This parable deals with the content of the heart as one prays. It serves as a lesson for all who come with the attitude of the Pharisee who comes before God prideful of his own abilities. He feels superior to others because in the eyes of the world, he is doing everything right. The dangerous thing about pride is we trust in our own abilities rather than God's. In addition, it leads us to look down on others whom God loves and who are created in God's own image.

Unfortunately, this has crept into the church, among Christians and in ministry. This parable serves to remind us that just because we may be ministers, it does not make us superior to those who are not; rather it shows that we are all in need of God's grace and mercy and He honors those who realize this truth. 'God, have mercy on me, a sinner', is not just a prayer for those who we look down upon, but for all of us.

Week 7-Monday

Writing a Prayer Journal

"You will keep in perfect peace all who trust in you, whose thoughts are fixed on you!" (Isaiah 26:3)

A prayer journal is a little different from a regular diary-type journal, although it is very easy to intertwine the two (I do). The idea behind the prayer journal is to focus on your conversations with God. You set aside some time every day to write about what is happening in your life. What makes it special is that it is written to the Lord, like one long prayer.

The prayer journal is not meant to be formal. It can contain your thoughts, feelings, hopes, and dreams. You can write it in the same way you would write a letter to a friend or along the same lines as a conversation, you would have with someone you can trust and confide in. God is interested in every aspect of our life, big and small, silly or solemn.

A prayer journal is a way to learn more about him, and to track where you have grown and been blessed as you read the pages. You can tell God about your day: what worries you, even what you have to remember to do. You can praise him, ask him questions about what to do or things you do not understand. You can place in writing your prayer requests for people you know in need, which can also help you to remember to pray for them again in the coming days.

Some people like to read devotions every day and write down what they learned or how it affected them. A prayer journal is also a great place for this. Others like to take their prayer journal to church or Bible study and jot down the points they want to remember. What you do and do not want to include is up to you. The main idea is to be open and honest, and to set aside that time as a part of your time with God. Daily, write down the prayers you offer up to him, including praises, desires, and hurts. You are writing letters to God and keeping up with them. In fact, you can even write your entries in letterform. The point is to keep up with what you are saying to him. Although it is very important to write down any prayer requests, the idea is to encompass that, but also to go beyond that.

When you write down your requests, you can later see how God is working in your life to answer those prayers, either divinely or naturally. Scripture states that when we ask for something in prayer, believing, then it will come to pass (Matthew 21:22). Writing down your praises helps to strengthen your expectancy in having your prayers answered. It focuses your attention on the positive things that God has already done in your life, and helps you understand how truly capable He is at answering your prayer.

Monitoring the hurts, the joys, and the concerns you have during the day also helps strengthen your walk with God. He often uses these things to get our attention or to switch our minds in a new direction. Writing these down, along with what caused them, allows us to go back later and see what God is doing in relation to them.

Keeping a prayer journal is one way to help you strengthen your relationship with God. It can help you to remain focused and aware of his presence with you. It may help you to lay down your burdens and to feel wrapped in the warmth of Gods loving arms.

So, try writing a prayer journal. What do you want to tell God? What do you want to ask of God? How would you like God to respond? Write it all down. What would you really like to say? God is waiting and listening for whatever you have to say? Remember, God loves you.

Week 7-Tuesday

God loves our enemies.

"If you love those who love you, what credit is that to you? Even 'sinners' love those who love them. And if you do good to those who are good to you, what credit is that to you? Even 'sinners' do that. And if you lend to those from whom you expect repayment, what credit is that to you? Even 'sinners' lend to 'sinners,' expecting to be repaid in full. But love your enemies, do good to them, and lend to them without expecting to get anything back. Then your reward will be great, and you will be sons of the Most High, because he is kind to the ungrateful and wicked. Be merciful, just as your Father is merciful. (Luke 6:32-40)

That is quite a tall order, but no one ever said that being Christian was going to be easy.

I was in a bible study class last night and the subject of God's people. We sometimes forget this, but all people are God's people. It is just that some choose to recognize that and some do not. Consequently, we are all connected. We are even connected to those who we do not really like. Sometimes it is difficult to remember that. We want God to be on our side. We want God to help us prevail over our enemies.

Think about it, God does not choose to have enemies. People choose to have enemies. We look at people and immediately put them into some type of box and label them. Those we have great affiliation with, we sometimes call friends. Those who we have great difficulties with, we sometimes call enemies. We may not like those people who do not look like us, or act like us, or think like us. God does not look at his people that way. God has even allowed his people to disagree with him by allowing for "free will." Do we allow others to have free will?

We are all loved by God in our various shapes, sizes, colors, levels of intelligence, and varying gifts. The test of our Christianity is to try to love each other and see each other in the same way God sees us.

Week 7-Wednesday

Remember the Sabbath

We can see what Jesus meant by looking at the phrase:

"The Sabbath was made for man, not man for the Sabbath" (Mark 2:27).

His point was that the Sabbath was made to serve people, instead of people being created to serve the Sabbath. The Sabbath was a servant, not a master. He was addressing the relative importance of the Sabbath, and how the Sabbath should be a day for both rest from the Week's labor and service to others.

Sabbath can be a far-reaching revolutionary tool for cultivating those precious human qualities that grow only in time.

Remember the Sabbath means:

1. Remember that everything that you have received is a blessing from God.
2. Remember to delight in your life and in the fruits of your labor.
3. Remember to stop and offer thanks to God for all the good things in your life.

The Sabbath is not only for ourselves; rested and refreshed; we more generously serve all those who need our care. The human spirit is naturally generous; the instant we are filled, our first impulse is to be useful, to be kind, and to give something away.

The practice of Sabbath, is designed specifically to restore us, a gift of time in which we allow the cares and concerns of the marketplace to fall away. We set aside time to delight in being alive, to savor the gifts of all creation, and to give thanks to God for the blessings we may have missed in our necessary preoccupation with our work.

Honesty, courage, kindness, civility, wisdom, compassion—these can only be nourished in the soil of time and attention, and need experience and practice to come to harvest. These are not commodities that can be bought, sold, or invested. They cannot be manufactured, advertised, or marketed. Our core human values, the deepest and best of who we are, require the nourishment of time and care, if we are to grow and flourish.

What are some of the precepts that guide your life?
To follow Jesus?
To be kind?
To be grateful?
To be honest?
To serve your neighbor?
To help the earth?
To love children?
Make a list of principles that shape your days. Include those you currently follow and those you would like to follow. On Sabbath, take time to speak them aloud. Notice how you feel when you hear them. What resistance or relief arises? Notice how the memory of these spoken precepts resonates in your body throughout the day. Love, too, requires rest: unstructured moments of intimate companionship, seeing, touching, and being with. Our presence and attention are the tangible manifestations of true love.

Sabbath is an incubator for wisdom. When we allow the rush and pressure of our days to fall away, even for a short period of time, we are more able to discern the essential truth of what lies before us.

Without stillness, without being present, we will get it all wrong.

Three biggest temptations:
To be useful
To be important
To be powerful

At our best, we become Sabbath for one another. We are the emptiness, the day of rest. We become space, that our loved ones, the lost and sorrowful, may find rest in us.

Therefore, remember the Sabbath as not necessarily a day, but a place to grow in God's service to others and us.

Week 7-Thursday

More on the Good News

Loving Spirit of Wisdom,
guide our thoughts and our memories.
In the light of your love,
may we see what is important for us to remember,
what is important for us to hold to our hearts,
and what we need simply to let go of in peace.
For we trust you to be our guide
even when the path seems unclear to us.
Through Jesus Christ,
Amen.

After living in Nazareth for thirty years (Luke 3:23), Jesus began to deliver His message, which was called the Good News (Matthew 4:23). What was the Good News? In the time of Jesus, the people were burdened with laws that regulated the smallest layers of daily life. Besides the oppressive laws of their Roman conquerors, there was the body of Jewish law. There were not just Ten Commandments; there were 613 commandments and 365 prohibitions. When they could not measure up to the laws, the religious leaders cut them off from the society of decent people.

Jesus told people He had come to fulfill that prophecy, to bring them the Good News for which they had waited for so long (Luke 4:20-21). Part of the Good News brought to us by Jesus was that being fully human in the true sense of the word was true holiness. No commandments and prohibitions made one holy. Being what God created us to be, just ourselves, good human beings was what made one holy (Mark 4:35-41). There is a profound revelation in that, and an important part of the Good News, that you could be ordinary, doing the ordinary, everyday things that people do, and underneath that simple, ordinary persona, possess extraordinary holiness.

How Jesus lived His own life as a human shows how we are to live ours (John 16:25-28). In His own life, Jesus lived simply. He was deeply in love with everything and everyone living, from God down to the simplest creature. He was gentle and compassionate, especially to those who were ostracized by society (Mark 2:17). He never gave an appearance of self-righteousness, but had a genuine humility and meekness and an understanding of others.

It is revealing that Jesus chose a wedding party for the launch of His public ministry (John 2:1-11). The news of what he did probably spread like wildfire, alerting everyone in the surrounding area to His kindness and His remarkable gift to the bride and groom. Kindness seems to be the message that Jesus wanted to precede Him, to disarm people so that they would not fear Him. Everything about Jesus spoke of simplicity, being born in a stable, living an unknown existence, showing nothing out of the ordinary except when some need called forth His extraordinary power to heal or to comfort.

Today as we go through our day, we should think about how we proclaim the "Good News." How do we heal? How do we comfort?

Week 7-Friday

Is awareness important?

9For what I do is not the good I want to do; no, the evil I do not want to do—this I keep on doing. Now if I do what I do not want to do, it is no longer I who do it, but it is sin living in me that does it. (Romans 7:9)

Paul is telling us in this passage, that doing good can be very difficult. Sometimes the more we try to do what is good, the easier it is to do what is bad. So, some may ask, what is the point? I think that the point that Paul is trying to make is that in trying to "go it alone" without God's help, we will fail. As long as we are aware of this, not all is lost. God is always there to give us strength when we are at our weakest. However, there has to be that awareness. We have to be aware that we are truly helpless without God. In our pride, we think that we are in control of our lives. However, our sense of awareness tells us that we are not.

I think that God is asking all of us to develop a sense of awareness so that we first, know when we have failed to do what is good, and second, to know that we must rely on God's assistance to help us in our weakness. Perfection is not what God wants from us. God wants us to have an awareness that we are always in need of his assistance.

I think that we can always rest in the knowledge that God will be there for us in our time of need.

Week 7-Saturday

Prayer to live in God's Presence
Dear God,
You have promised to remain forever with those
who do what is just and right.
Help me to live in your presence.
The loving plan of Your Wisdom was made known when
Jesus, your Son, became man like us.
I want to obey Jesus commandment of love
and bring your peace and joy to others.
Keep before me the wisdom and love
you have made known in Your Son, Jesus.
Help me to be like Him in word and deed.

Let us all continue to live in the presence of God, and renew this prayer each day of our lives. May God help us to continue to bring his Kingdom to all we encounter throughout our day.

Week 7-Sunday

God is not the source of temptation

"No one experiencing temptation should say 'I am being tempted by God'; for God is not subject to temptation to evil, and he himself tempts no one. Rather, each person is tempted when lured and enticed by his desire" (James 1:13-15).

I was so glad that I came upon this reading today. It has always troubled me that God would tempt us into sin. Would any parent do that to their beloved child? Would anyone try to lure his or her beloved into a trap?

In this reading, James says that God tempts no one. However, rather, we are tempted by our own desires. This makes a lot more sense than God trying to trap us. That would not be the act of a loving God. It might be the act of Satan to tempt us, but without any outside influences, we are tempted by many things. God is there as our protector, but will not step in unless we ask for his assistance.

Repeatedly we see that the message is that we cannot rely upon ourselves to always do the right thing. We need God to be helping us. We need to rely on God. That may be very ego deflating to some people. Lots of us tend to want to think that we can handle anything on our own. We need no one's help until we find out that we are not really in control. We should not feel alone in this, because no one else is in control either, except God.

I am happy that James told me in the reading today that God is not going to tempt me to go after what will be bad for me, just to see if I do. I do not need any help in going after the wrong thing; I do that pretty well on my own. God is there to help me to do what is right and to go after the things that will be good for me. That gives me great consolation, even in times of trouble. God will always be there to help me along to the right road, the right side, to the right desire. I can trust that God will not put blocks and temptations in my way to help me follow the wrong path. My only trouble is that I need to remember to ask for help when I need it and that help will be there for me.

God is there for you as well.

Week 8-Monday

Religion vs. Spirituality

[3]For by the grace given me I say to every one of you: Do not think of yourself more highly than you ought, but rather think of yourself with sober judgment, in accordance with the measure of faith God has given you. [4]Just as each of us has one body with many members, and these members do not all have the same function, [5]so in Christ we who are many form one body, and each member belongs to all the others. [6]We have different gifts, according to the grace given us. If a man's gift is prophesying, let him use it in proportion to his[b] faith. [7]If it is serving, let him serve; if it is teaching, let him teach; [8]if it is encouraging, let him encourage; if it is contributing to the needs of others, let him give generously; if it is leadership, let him govern diligently; if it is showing mercy, let him do it cheerfully. (Romans 12:3-8)

It is common to find individuals who have a negative attitude toward formal religion, but do have a positive attitude to what they refer to as spirituality. The difference they express is that they see formal religion as an overpowering presence; whereas spirituality is the experience of God as an overpowering presence. In other words, formal religion, instead of being a way to connect with God and others, becomes a barrier to that connectivity. Spirituality is an opening toward the experience of interconnectedness, which forms the world. God is the overpowering presence within us that is reaching toward us through our connectedness.

Many of those who acknowledge their spirituality, while at the same time reject formal religion, are expressing a preference for this empowering sense of the divine presence. They believe that spiritually overcomes the distance that is often established by formal religion, between oneself and God. They believe that spirituality alone encourages an understanding that God is closer to home than we tend to find with traditional religion. God is not out there, but present at the very center of self. We can experience God, not by leaving the human condition behind, but by entering fully into the richness of all that humanity can be.

However, is individual spirituality enough to be able to experience that richness? The interdependency, which forms the world, especially our human need for one another opens an aspect of our everyday lives, which we very much take for granted. Religion should work to foster this connectedness and interdependency. We do not realize how interconnected we are, nor how much we rely on each other for care and assistance. Unless you are an auto mechanic, you cannot make your car run when it breaks down. Unless you are a plumber, you cannot fix a faucet when it breaks. Unless you are a pilot, you cannot fly yourself from one place to another.

The spiritual dimension of human experience should not only awaken the awareness of the reality of our connectedness, but also demonstrate it by how we interact and care for one another. In the light of that care, the lines, which separate and divide us from one another, from the world, and from God, fade to the point of disappearance. By associating this connectedness and care with the presence of God, we move beyond the dualism which otherwise sets apart God and the world, and sets apart God from humans. Spirituality is our openness to God and the world.

Formal religion should be the expression of our Christian spirituality and openness to God and to our community. Formal religion creates a common language of love both to God and to each other. Our Christian Spirituality is based upon community. We are connected to each other and to God. Religion is just the expression of that love in community. We should not look at religion as the object of love nor the object of our connectedness, but the voice of love and connectedness. I guess what I am saying, is we should not be afraid of formal religion.

We, as Christians, need formal religion to have a common voice and understanding to be able to share our spirituality with others. Christian spirituality needs to be celebrated within the community. If religion becomes more than the common voice of love for God and others, the purpose of religion has been missed. Jesus loved community and always surrounded himself with people. Jesus continues to share himself in community with us and wants us to be able share of ourselves with each other. Formal religion, when viewed as a voice of love and not an institution or prison, becomes our language of love.

We can pray alone in our rooms, and some of that is good. When we pray together in community, we become the "one body of Christ."

Week 8-Tuesday

Have you injured anyone with words today?

[2]We all stumble in many ways. If anyone is never at fault in what he says, he is a perfect man, able to keep his whole body in check.

[3]When we put bits into the mouths of horses to make them obey us, we can turn the whole animal. [4]Or take ships as an example. Although they are so large and are driven by strong winds, they are steered by a very small rudder wherever the pilot wants to go. [5]Likewise the tongue is a small part of the body, but it makes great boasts. Consider what a great forest is set on fire by a small spark. [6]The tongue also is a fire, a world of evil among the parts of the body. It corrupts the whole person, sets the whole course of his life on fire, and is itself set on fire by hell.

[7]All kinds of animals, birds, reptiles and creatures of the sea are being tamed and have been tamed by man, [8]but no man can tame the tongue. It is a restless evil, full of deadly poison.

[9]With the tongue we praise our Lord and Father, and with it we curse men, who have been made in God's likeness. [10]Out of the same mouth come praise and cursing. My brothers, this should not be. [11]Can both fresh water and salt water flow from the same spring? [12]My brothers, can a fig tree bear olives, or a grapevine bear figs? Neither can a salt spring produce fresh water. (James 3:2-12)

This passage in the letter of James calls our attention to our speech. When we speak, we need to be conscious of whether we build up the body of Christ or do we tear down the body of Christ. Do we help others to live, or do we kill them with our words? Sometimes being negative or gossiping are just bad habits we let ourselves get into. We sometimes speak without even thinking. It seems to be a matter of being unaware. Are we aware of our words? Do we think about them before we say them? Do we stop to reflect before saying something that can cause others hurt and shame? Do we destroy another's character because we can? All things to think about.

As children, we may have said, "sticks and stones can break my bones, but names can never hurt me." On the contrary, the bones will eventually heal, but the names can cause pain that will last a lifetime. Words can end relationships, drive people apart, and keep them that way.

I think it would be better to stop and think about what to say before it is said. It is better to just get into the habit of speaking positively about people. This becomes a choice for love rather than hate. Even if you feel that, the person does not deserve it, give them the benefit of the doubt, and be kind.

I try to choose my words carefully when I write this blog every day. Perhaps I do not always succeed, but I try.

Choose to build up the body of Christ, stay away from tearing down. Choose your words carefully.

Week 8-Wednesday

How can we Evangelize?

Each of us is called to invite others to turn toward God. Each of us can invite others to think more deeply about the meaning of their lives. Each of us can invite another to share our search for a deeper knowledge of the love of God. Each of us can invite another to pray. Each family can invite others to experience hospitality in their home that clearly flows from Christian love. Each of us can invite another to share a community experience or come to our parish Eucharistic celebration.

[18]Then Jesus came to them and said, "All authority in heaven and on earth has been given to me. [19]Therefore go and make disciples of all nations, baptizing them in[a] the name of the Father and of the Son and of the Holy Spirit, [20]and teaching them to obey everything I have commanded you. (Matthew 28:18-20)

Accepting the Word:

We cannot give what we have not first received.

[14]How, then, can they call on the one they have not believed in? And how can they believe in the one of whom they have not heard? And how can they hear without someone preaching to them? [15]And how can they preach unless they are sent? As it is written, "How beautiful are the feet of those who bring good news![] [16]But not all the Israelites accepted the good news. For Isaiah says, "Lord, who has believed our message?" [17]Consequently, faith comes from hearing the message, and the message is heard through the word of Christ. (Romans 10:14-17)

Each of us is called to a personal relationship with a God who loves us. Each of us needs to listen to God's Word as it is written in the Scriptures. Each of us, by the power of the Holy Spirit, must make a decision to surrender to God's love and to commit ourselves to follow Christ. Each of us needs the support of a faith community to experience God's love and empower us to go out to others.

[1]Again Jesus began to teach by the lake. The crowd that gathered
around him was so large that he got into a boat and sat in it out on the
lake, while all the people were along the shore at the water's edge. [2]He
taught them many things by parables, and in his teaching said:
[3]"Listen! A farmer went out to sow his seed. [4]As he was scattering the
seed, some fell along the path, and the birds came and ate it up. [5]Some
fell on rocky places, where it did not have much soil. It sprang up
quickly, because the soil was shallow. [6]But when the sun came up, the
plants were scorched, and they withered because they had no root.
[7]Other seed fell among thorns, which grew up and choked the plants,
so that they did not bear grain. [8]Still other seed fell on good soil. It
came up, grew and produced a crop, multiplying thirty, sixty, or even
a hundred times." [9]Then Jesus said, "He who has ears to hear, let him
hear." (Mark 4:1-9)

Living It Out:

Our lives speak more clearly than our words.

" Do not deceive yourselves by just listening to God's Word; instead, put it into practice ... For whoever looks closely into the perfect law that sets people free, who keeps on paying attention to it and does not simply listen and then forget it, but puts it into practice, that person will be blessed by God is what is done." (James 1:22-25)

Each of us is called to share the love we have received with others. Each of us can show care for each person we meet at work, on the street, and in times of leisure. Each of us who is a member of a family can express our love for each other within the family. As a family, we can show love toward others. Each faith community must let people know that they are Disciples of Christ by the love they have for one another. Each of us is called to help others as effectively as we can especially the poor and the marginalized.

[13]"You are the salt of the earth. But if the salt loses its saltiness, how can it be made salty again? It is no longer good for anything, except to be thrown out and trampled by men.
[14]"You are the light of the world. A city on a hill cannot be hidden. [15]Neither do people light a lamp and put it under a bowl. Instead, they put it on its stand, and it gives light to everyone in the house. [16]In the same way, let your light shine before men, that they may see your good deeds and praise your Father in heaven. (Matthew 5:13-16).

"Those who have received the Good News and who have been gathered by it into a community of salvation can and must communicate it and spread it..." (No. 13) (Evangelization in the Modern World, Pope Paul VI)

"It is unthinkable that a person should accept the word and give himself to the kingdom without becoming a person who bears witness to it and proclaims it in his turn." (No. 24) (Evangelization in the Modern World, Pope Paul VI.

Week 8-Thursday

Lead us away from temptation

[1]Jesus, full of the Holy Spirit, returned from the Jordan and was led by the Spirit in the desert, [2]where for forty days he was tempted by the devil. He ate nothing during those days, and at the end of them, he was hungry.

[3]The devil said to him, "If you are the Son of God, tell this stone to become bread."

[4]Jesus answered, "It is written: 'Man does not live on bread alone.'"

[5]The devil led him up to a high place and showed him in an instant all the kingdoms of the world. [6]And he said to him, "I will give you all their authority and splendor, for it has been given to me, and I can give it to anyone I want to. [7]So if you worship me, it will all be yours."

[8]Jesus answered, "It is written: 'Worship the Lord your God and serve him only.'"

[9]The devil led him to Jerusalem and had him stand on the highest point of the temple. "If you are the Son of God," he said, "throw yourself down from here. [10]For it is written:

"'He will command his angels concerning you to guard you carefully; 11they will lift you up in their hands, so that you will not strike your foot against a stone.'"

[12]Jesus answered, "It says: 'Do not put the Lord your God to the test.'"

[13]When the devil had finished all this tempting, he left him until an opportune time. (Lk 4:1-13).

In reading, the Holy Spirit leads Jesus into the wilderness for forty days. While he is there, Jesus is tempted by the devil. Luke describes the temptations as the three most alluring temptations of his day: love of pleasure, love of riches, and love of power. Jesus resists the devil, which gives witness to how followers of Christ are to deal with temptation.

This reading also has Jewish roots. The Israelites wandered forty years in the desert after God delivered them from Egypt. They were tested with hunger, the lure of false Gods, and the temptation to test God. Jesus experienced the very same temptations and unlike many of the Israelites before him, he responded to each of them out of faithfulness to God. Jesus relies completely on God when confronted with temptation and in doing so; he reverses the human infidelity of history.

So what tempts us? Probably the same things as in the ancient world, love of pleasure, love of riches, and love of power. How do we overcome these temptations? The answer is "Trust in God." Ask for Gods help when faced with the temptations you experience each day. In the end, giving in to these temptations will not bring happiness. Sometimes, in the giving in to our temptations, we are faced with bigger problems than if we had resisted them. If we place ourselves in God's hands, we have to have faith that God knows what we need and will take care of those needs.

Week 8-Friday

How do we love?

"A new command I give you: Love one another. As I have loved you, so you must love one another. By this all men will know that you are my disciples, if you love one another (John 13:34-35).

Remember when you were a kid and your mom or dad would say, "Now be nice to your brother or sister." In addition, you might not say it but you were at least thinking, "Why? He/she is not being nice to me. It isn't fair that I have to be kind to them when they're being mean to me."

As a believer in Christ, at times your Heavenly Father says the same thing to you, "Be nice to your brother..." Our human tendency is to shout, "No! I do not want to! Even though he is a Christian, he is not treating me nicely. It isn't fair that I have to be kind to him when he is being mean to me." Still Jesus says, "Be kind to one another." In fact, He goes o far as to say, "Love one another as I have loved you." And when you ask, "Why," He replies, "So others will see that you follow me."

The mark of a Christian is that the love of Christ in the lives of believers is what sets them apart from the world. He concludes that the world has a right to judge the authenticity of Christ's claims to be the Messiah, the Savior, the Son of God, by what they see in the lives of His followers. Was He the One who could change lives? Are the lives of His followers different from those of the world? Do they truly love one another in difficult times?

Loving one another includes being willing to respectfully confront one another when necessary, to work to find solutions to disagreements, and to forgive those who hurt you. That means giving up your desire to be angry and to get back at the offender. The secret lies in abiding in Christ.

Beloved Jesus, make me ever mindful that the world is watching my life. Guide my thoughts and guard my lips when feelings of hurt and fear overtake me. Let me show love to my brothers and sisters so that others will say, “Truly Christ can change a life. Surely He is the Son of God.”

Week 8-Saturday

Cleanliness is next to Godliness!

1The Pharisees and some of the teachers of the law who had come
from Jerusalem gathered around Jesus and 2saw some of his disciples
eating food with hands that were "unclean," that is, unwashed. 3(The
Pharisees and all the Jews do not eat unless they give their hands a
ceremonial washing, holding to the tradition of the elders. 4When they
come from the marketplace they do not eat unless they wash. And they
observe many other traditions, such as the washing of cups, pitchers
and kettles.])

5So the Pharisees and teachers of the law asked Jesus, "Why don't your disciples live according to the tradition of the elders instead of eating their food with 'unclean' hands?"

6He replied, "Isaiah was right when he prophesied about you hypocrites; as it is written:

" 'These people honor me with their lips, but their hearts are far from me.

7They worship me in vain;

their teachings are but rules taught by men.' 8You have let go of the
commands of God and are holding on to the traditions of men."

9And he said to them: "You have a fine way of setting aside the
commands of God in order to observe[c your own traditions! 10For
Moses said, 'Honor your father and your mother,'[d] and, 'Anyone who
curses his father or mother must be put to death.'[e] 11But you say that if
a man says to his father or mother: 'Whatever help you might otherwise
have received from me is Corban' (that is, a gift devoted to God), 12then
you no longer let him do anything for his father or mother. 13Thus you
nullify the word of God by your tradition that you have handed down.
And you do many things like that."

[14]Again Jesus called the crowd to him and said, "Listen to me, everyone, and understand this. [15]Nothing outside a man can make him 'unclean' by going into him. Rather, it is what comes out of a man that makes him 'unclean.' "[f]

[17]After he had left the crowd and entered the house, his disciples asked him about this parable. [18]"Are you so dull?" he asked. "Don't you see that nothing that enters a man from the outside can make him 'unclean'? [19]For it doesn't go into his heart but into his stomach, and then out of his body." (In saying this, Jesus declared all foods "clean.")

[20]He went on: "What comes out of a man is what makes him 'unclean.' [21]For from within, out of men's hearts, come evil thoughts, sexual immorality, theft, murder, adultery, [22]greed, malice, deceit, lewdness, envy, slander, arrogance and folly. [23]All these evils come from inside and make a man 'unclean.' "

(Mark 7:1-23)

Jesus was telling his disciples that to be clean means to have a heart that is loving. I think sometime that we, too, are caught up in our own religious rituals without giving any thought as to why we are doing them. Do we meet God in these rituals? Alternatively, is it just something we have been told to do? Do we perform these rituals with joy?

On the other hand, are we doing them for worldly acclaim?

I think that Jesus was telling us that if our heart is not in the religious rituals they do not mean much. If we do not care for one another and love one another, all the rituals in the world will not make us clean. It is something to think about. We need to reflect on our lives. What are we doing? Are we performing mindless rituals, or are we really in touch with the will of God. Are we developing our relationship with God or are we just going through the motions? Talk to God today. Ask God what he wants you to do.

Then listen for the answer. There will be one.

Week 8-Sunday

Have you talked to God today?

"My prayer is not for them alone. I pray also for those who will believe in me through their message, that all of them may be one, Father, just as you are in me and I am in you" (John 17:20-21).

Jesus prayed in praise to God, the Father—"At that time Jesus, full of joy through the Holy Spirit, said, 'I praise you, Father, lord of heaven and earth, because you have hidden these things from the wise and learned, and revealed them to little children. Yes, Father, for this was your good pleasure'" (Luke 10:21).

Jesus prayed prayers of thanksgiving—"*While they were eating, Jesus took bread, gave thanks and broke it, and gave it to his disciples, saying, 'Take it; this is my body'" (Mark 14:22).*

Jesus prayed in a posture and with an attitude of reverent submission—*"Going a little farther, he fell with his face to the ground and prayed, 'My Father, if it is possible, may this cup be taken from me. Yet not as I will, but as you will'" (Matthew 26:39).*

Jesus prayed in times of anguish—*"And being in anguish, he prayed more earnestly, and his sweat was like drops of blood falling to the ground" (Luke 22:44).*

"*About the ninth hour Jesus cried out in a loud voice, 'Eloi, Eloi, lama sabachthani?'—which means, "My God, my God, why have you forsaken me?'" (Matthew 27:46).*

"Teach us to pray," was the request of the disciples to Jesus. They confessed that they were not able to pray on their own. God wants to communicate with us and wants us to communicate with Him. Just as communication is important for us to develop our human relationships, our relationship with God requires communication as well. Prayer is our way to communicate with God. However, prayer does not always have to be in the form of canned prayers or even in words alone. There are many other forms of prayer.

Things to Do to Communicate with God:

• Sing to God
• Listen to worship music and sing along
• Go for a walk with God
• Journal in a notebook to God
• Study the Scriptures with Him
• Listen to Bible reading on tape
• Take a nap with Him
• At night study the stars with Him
• Write out your prayer as a love letter to God
• Listen to a good sermon
• Read a book on prayer or God's person
• Go for a bike ride in His creation
• Eat a great meal thanking Him for every good thing
• Have a quiet conversation with a friend about Him
• Go fishing with God at your side • Evaluate your life and ministry with God looking on
• Have a coffee break with God
• Memorize a Scriptural Promise He gives you
• Plan your future goals with his advice
• Meditate on the Names of God
• Watch a bird, stare at the waves, study a bug
• Meditate on the Cross
• Meditate on God's Creation
• Read the Prayers of the Bible
• Play an Instrument to the Lord
• Do a New Testament Word Study

We know that God is always present with us. Prayer is communication with God as we turn our hearts, minds, spirits, and thoughts toward Him. Prayer is a form of worship. We bow before our awesome God with a humble and contrite heart. We bring God our adoration in prayer and praise to Him.

We also seek and find, ask and receive, knock and have opened to us (Matt. 7:7-8).

Have you talked to God today?

Week 9-Monday

On the Journey
13Now that same day two of them were going to a village called
Emmaus, about seven miles from Jerusalem. 14They were talking with
each other about everything that had happened. 15As they talked and
discussed these things with each other, Jesus himself came up and
walked along with them; 16but they were kept from recognizing him.

17He asked them, "What are you discussing together as you walk
along?"
They stood still, their faces downcast. 18One of them, named
Cleopas, asked him, "Are you only a visitor to Jerusalem and do not
know the things that have happened there in these days?"

19"What things?" he asked.
"About Jesus of Nazareth," they replied. "He was a prophet,
powerful in word and deed before God and all the people. 20The chief
priests and our rulers handed him over to be sentenced to death, and
they crucified him; 21but we had hoped that he was the one who was
going to redeem Israel. And what is more, it is the third day since all
this took place. 22In addition, some of our women amazed us. They went
to the tomb early this morning 23but didn't find his body. They came and
told us that they had seen a vision of angels, who said he was alive.
24Then some of our companions went to the tomb and found it just as the
women had said, but him they did not see."

25He said to them, "How foolish you are, and how slow of heart to
believe all that the prophets have spoken! 26Did not the Christ have to
suffer these things and then enter his glory?" 27And beginning with
Moses and all the Prophets, he explained to them what was said in all
the Scriptures concerning himself.

28 *As they approached the village to which they were going, Jesus
acted as if he were going farther.* 29 *But they urged him strongly, "Stay
with us, for it is nearly evening; the day is almost over." So he went in
to stay with them.*

30 *When he was at the table with them, he took bread, gave thanks,
broke it and began to give it to them.* 31 *Then their eyes were opened and
they recognized him, and he disappeared from their sight.* 32 *They asked
each other, "Were not our hearts burning within us while he talked
with us on the road and opened the Scriptures to us?"*

33 *They got up and returned at once to Jerusalem. There they found
the Eleven and those with them, assembled together. (Luke 24:13-33)*

For the Journey, we turn to Luke's Gospel for his unique resurrection story. Two of Jesus' followers, who failed to see Him in the breaking up of their personal hopes and failed to see Him in the breaking up of His companions, will now recognize Him "in the breaking of the bread."

As a "companion," literally, "with-bread," is how Jesus comes alongside these two dispirited disciples. Their heads are down and they see the earth without any hope for the new life they had sought in the teachings of Jesus. As a companion, He joins their darkness and gently leads them through their reflections on what has recently happened in Jerusalem. Their eyes are dimmer than their spirits and they find it hard to believe what they saw happen and what they have heard about His Resurrection. They did not see it happen, so for them, it did not really occur.

We watch and listen to their sharing in the rising of Jesus as their hearts burn within them while they listen to this mysterious companion. He is a "collector," a "finder" and He has risen to raise both those who seek for Him and those who take the road back to Emmaus.

We find comfort and great joy in watching Jesus compassionately go out after those who have their hearts and hopes broken. It is so human to doubt and want to turn towards where ever our Emmaus hiding place may be. They freely turned to their own tombs burying their frustrated plans and fractured friendships. Our self-chosen tombs can be such comfortable resting places. These men are going back, and in meeting Jesus, they will want, not to go back, but to return.

We have been praying often about our own tombs and hiding places. Their walls of fear, the locked doors of self-negativity and regret, have been abandoned and yet we know their comforts and the easily found roads back to their ever-opened portals. It is very dark in our tombs and Jesus constantly invites us into the sunshine. The word "consolation" literally means, "with the sunshine" and conversely, "desolation" means "down out of the sunshine."

The men we watch this day experience the warmth of the sun in their being invited out of their darkness. We pray this day with the joys of having been found, having been called out into the sunshine. We also pray with the joy in the awareness that He will always be collecting His followers in the breaking up of their hearts and hopes. He has risen so that we might have confidence in His grace more than our fragile selves.

Dear Jesus,

We read the story of the men on the road to Emmaus. We shake our heads and wonder, how could they see you, someone they love and trust so much, and then not even recognize you? We would certainly recognize you…wouldn't we?

We feel like we have been through so much together. How could we not see you? Well, except maybe when we are worried about how successful, we are or how we look to others. Alternatively, wondering why we have to speak up about injustices to the poor when we are so busy already. We know we fail to be our best self so often, and we know how often you are there in that failure to forgive and support.

Week 9-Tuesday

Who will believe what has not been shared?

"I hear of your love and of the faith which you have in the Lord Jesus and in all the saints, and I pray that the sharing of your faith may promote the knowledge of all the good that is ours in Christ. For I have derived much joy and comfort from your love because the hearts of God's people have been refreshed by you." (Philemon 1:4-7)

Each of us is called to share the Good News we have heard and believed. Each of us can tell others of the ways that we have experienced God in our lives. Each of us needs to listen with respect to each other's story of faith. Each of us can speak of these faith stories to each other as family and as a large Christian community. Each of us must share our faith, our hope, and our love with those who have not heard about or do not experience these gifts of God.

Each of us is called to share our faith. We can no longer leave this work to the ordained, vowed, religious, and church professionals. The mission of the laity in the workplace, the home, in social settings, and in the political arena is to proclaim and share the Good News. Take some time to reflect on the four elements of the evangelization cycle by looking at your own life experience in relation to the scriptures. Discover your own response to the call to evangelize.

Share your story of God's love with others.

Week 9-Wednesday

The Holy Spirit is promised to all of us.

4On one occasion, while he was eating with them, he gave them this command: "Do not leave Jerusalem, but wait for the gift my Father promised, which you have heard me speak about. 5For John baptized with water, but in a few days you will be baptized with the Holy Spirit."

6So when they met together, they asked him, "Lord, are you at this time going to restore the kingdom to Israel?"

7He said to them: "It is not for you to know the times or dates the Father has set by his own authority. 8But you will receive power when the Holy Spirit comes on you; and you will be my witnesses in Jerusalem, and in all Judea and Samaria, and to the ends of the earth." (Acts: 1:4-8)

• being assembled together with them. Jesus often communed with His friends and disciples over a meal: at the feeding of the five thousand, with tax collectors and sinners, at the Pharisee's house, at the Last Supper, and after the Resurrection

• wait for the Promise of the Father. The Holy Spirit was the gift of the Father and the gift of Jesus the Son

• not many days from now. A few days would pass before Pentecost

• at this time restore the kingdom to Israel. From what Jesus said in Matt. 19:28, the disciples thought that He might overthrow the Romans and restore the physical kingdom to Israel

• Holy Spirit has come upon you. Jesus means that the Holy Spirit will show His control of their lives with visible manifestations: the blowing of a violent wind, the appearance of tongues of fire, and speaking in foreign languages

• witnesses to Me in Jerusalem, and in all Judea and Samaria, and to the end of the earth. The book of Acts follows this strategy. The Jerusalem witness in chapter 2 gives in miniature form God's worldwide ministry: the "Jews…from every nation" (2:5) who heard and believed carried the message far and wide. In the rest of Acts the gospel spreads to Jerusalem (3:1-8:1), to Judea and Samaria, up to Antioch of Syria (8:1-12:25), and to the ends of the earth (13:1-28:31)

The Trinity is a description of the unique relationship of God the Father, the Son, and the Holy Spirit. If Jesus had stayed on earth, his physical presence would have limited the spread of the gospel, for physically he could be in only one place at a time. After his ascension, he would be spiritually present everywhere through the Holy Spirit. The Holy Spirit was sent so God would be with and within his followers after Jesus returned to heaven. His Spirit would comfort them, guide them to know his truth, remind them of Jesus' words, give them the right words to say, and fill them with power.

Jesus wants to fill all of us with his Spirit just as he did for the Apostles on Pentecost. Just ask Jesus to be with you as you begin your day. Some amazing things could happen.

Week 9-Thursday

Be Welcoming to Others

"7Accept one another, then, just as Christ accepted you, in order to bring praise to God. 8For I tell you that Christ has become a servant of the Jews on behalf of God's truth, to confirm the promises made to the patriarchs 9so that the Gentiles may glorify God for his mercy, as it is written:

"Therefore I will praise you among the Gentiles;
I will sing hymns to your name." 10Again, it says,
"Rejoice, O Gentiles, with his people." 11And again,
"Praise the Lord, all you Gentiles,
and sing praises to him, all you peoples." 12And again, Isaiah says,
"The Root of Jesse will spring up,
one who will arise to rule over the nations;
the Gentiles will hope in him."

13May the God of hope, fill you with all joy and peace, as you trust in him, so that you may overflow with hope by the power of the Holy Spirit. (Romans 15:7-13)

We can be welcoming to others by giving them the welcome of a listening heart. Each of us is called to invite others to turn toward God. Each of us can invite others to think more deeply about the meaning of their lives. Each of us can invite another to share our search for a deeper knowledge of the love of God. Each of us can invite another to pray. Each family can invite others to experience hospitality in their home that clearly flows from Christian love. Each of us can invite another to share a community experience or come to our parish Eucharistic celebration.

Who would you invite?

Week 9-Friday

Finding Inner Peace

"Peace I leave with you; my peace I give you. I do not give to you as the world gives. Do not let your hearts be troubled and do not be afraid"(John 14:27).

20 Tips for inner peace.

1. Learn to let go of the past.
2. Live for today.
3. Don't sweat the little things, and 99% of everything is little if you view it that way.
4. Find quiet time for yourself every single day without fail. You deserve it.
5. Raise your awareness level. Look at flowers, the sunset, your kids at play…
6. Spend time with peaceful people in peaceful places.
7. Eliminate every stressor that you possibly can from your life.
8. Find something that you enjoy doing and do it, even if you think you may not look dignified while you do it.
9. Laugh a lot every day.
10. Count your blessings every night before you go to sleep.
11. Find some grass and sit in it. Lean your back against a tree. Listen to the birds singing and daydream.
12. Read peaceful books, listen to peaceful music and play peaceful games.
13. Learn, for once and for all, that no one can disturb your peace unless you allow them to.
14. Forget trying to control others, it will never work.
15. Establish a dialogue with God. Talk to the Creator and listen for the reply.
16. Tell every single person that you care about how you feel.
17. Forgive any and every one who has ever hurt you.
18. Let go of expectations.

19. Stop and think before you talk. You will spend a lot less time having to eat your words.

20. Make today be the best day possible , and the future will take care of itself one day at a time.

Peace be with you!

Week 9-Saturday

Never Lose Hope

Before Jesus died he told his apostles "[33]"*I have told you these things, so that in me you may have peace. In this world you will have trouble. But take heart! I have overcome the world." (John 16:33)*

Hope is something you can never afford to lose. With hope, you always have a path towards peace. Whenever we are too stressed out and overwhelmed within our own life, we forget that hope. We forget that the sun always shines after a rainy day, and that this is merely a bump in the road. I find immense peace in just knowing, deep within my heart, that everything will be ok because Jesus is with me. With hope and trust in Jesus, I know that whatever is seemingly terrible is only temporary and that soon enough, things will be just fine. This lifts off all of that negativity from my entire being, and I feel better instantly.

When all seems to be hopeless, we need to pray. There are many times when we cannot face our problems on our own. Jesus is there to help us through these trying times. We cannot trust that the world will contain the answers for us. We cannot always trust others to help us, because everyone has their own problems. Jesus is there to carry us when we seem to be without hope.

Keep the following in mind:

Footprints in the Sand

One night I dreamed I was walking along the beach with the Lord. Many scenes from my life flashed across the sky.

In each scene, I noticed footprints in the sand. Sometimes there were two sets of footprints, other times there was one only.

This bothered me because I noticed that during the low periods of my life, when I was suffering from anguish, sorrow, or defeat, I could see only one set of footprints, so I said to the Lord,

"You promised me Lord,

that if I followed you, you would walk with me always. However, I have noticed that during the most trying periods of my life there has only been one set of footprints in the sand. Why, when I needed you most, have you not been there for me?"

The Lord replied, "The years when you have seen only one set of footprints, my child, is when I carried you."

Mary Stevenson, 1936

Week 9-Sunday

The Holy Spirit is promised for us all.

[1]When the day of Pentecost came, they were all together in one place. [2]Suddenly a sound like the blowing of a violent wind came from heaven and filled the whole house where they were sitting. [3]They saw what seemed to be tongues of fire that separated and came to rest on each of them. [4]All of them were filled with the Holy Spirit and began to speak in other tongues as the Spirit enabled them. (Acts 2:1-4)

Jesus instructed his disciples to witness to people of all nations about him. But they were told to wait first for the Holy Spirit. God has important work for us to do for him, but we must do it by the power of his Spirit. We often like to get on with the job, even if it means running ahead of God. But waiting is sometimes part of God's plan. Are you waiting and listening for God's complete instructions, or are you running ahead of his plans? We need God's timing and power to be truly effective.

The Spirit marks the beginning of the Christian experience. We cannot belong to Christ without his Spirit; we cannot be united to Christ without his Spirit; we cannot be adopted as his children without his Spirit; we cannot be in the body of Christ except by baptism in the Spirit. The Spirit is the power of our new lives. He begins a lifelong process of change as we become more like Christ. When we receive Christ by faith, we begin a personal relationship with God. The Holy Spirit works in us to help us become more like Christ.

Listen today. What is God saying to you?

Week 10-Monday

Live in the present moment

[25]"Therefore I tell you, do not worry about your life, what you will eat or drink; or about your body, what you will wear. Is not life more important than food, and the body more important than clothes? [26]Look at the birds of the air; they do not sow or reap or store away in barns, and yet your heavenly Father feeds them. Are you not much more valuable than they? [27]Who of you by worrying can add a single hour to his life?

[28]"And why do you worry about clothes? See how the lilies of the field grow. They do not labor or spin. [29]Yet I tell you that not even Solomon in all his splendor was dressed like one of these. [30]If that is how God clothes the grass of the field, which is here today and tomorrow is thrown into the fire, will he not much more clothe you, O you of little faith? [31]So do not worry, saying, 'What shall we eat?' or 'What shall we drink?' or 'What shall we wear?' [32]For the pagans run after all these things and your heavenly Father knows that you need them. [33]But seek first his kingdom and his righteousness and all these things will be given to you as well. [34]Therefore do not worry about tomorrow, for tomorrow will worry about itself. Each day has enough trouble of its own. (Matthew 6:25-34)

A lot of the time, what we are angry about is caused by worry about something we may have no control of. What we worry about is relating to something either in the past, or to something that has not happened. Living in the present moment erases all such thoughts. Why worry about something in the past that we cannot ever change? Why worry about something that we are not even sure will happen or not? This is why in the present moment you find true inner peace.

In the present moment, there are no problems and no concerns. There is only stillness, and it is within that stillness that you can uncover peace. I used to be such a person that worried all the time, to the point where I had trouble sleeping. Once I learned to live in the present moment, I stopped thinking about the past and any potential problems that may have occurred and allow the future to unfold as God wishes. God wants us to live every moment with joy. The past is gone, the future is uncertain, but the present is a gift. Why do you think it is called a present?

Week 10-Tuesday

Jesus provides a great example to us

"12When he had finished washing their feet, he put on his clothes and returned to his place. " Do you understand what I have done for you?" he asked them. 13"You call me 'Teacher' and 'Lord,' and rightly so, for that is what I am. 14Now that I, your Lord and Teacher, have washed your feet, you also should wash one another's feet. 15I have set you an example that you should do as I have done for you. 16I tell you the truth, no servant is greater than his master, nor is a messenger greater than the one who sent him. 17Now that you know these things; you will be blessed if you do them". (John 13:12-17)

As we have so often been taught, washing another's feet is an act of humility when we perform it as Christ instructs us. While it indeed should be done with a humble attitude, after a more intensive study of Christ's instructions concerning it, we will find a deeper and more meaningful reason why it is so vital that we do it with a correct understanding. This deeper meaning will help us realize how important Christ's example is to us today.

At first, it may also seem strange that, while the other three gospel writers focus on the bread and wine that Christ instituted that same evening—and make no mention of foot washing—John does just the opposite. We must remember that John, as the last of the gospel writers, fills in some of Jesus' acts and statements that the others left out of their gospels. The answer could be as simple as that John felt that the foot washing ceremony needed to be included in the New Testament canon. On the other hand, John probably recognized the direct connection between foot washing and the awesome work of Christ in His life, death, and afterlife.

The foot washing ceremony, recorded in John 13:1-17, allows us a window into the character of Jesus. When we apply the lessons of this unique and instructive ritual in our lives, it gives us a better understanding of why some people struggle to find happiness yet never fully achieve it, and why others lives are running over with joy. The ability to be of service to another is a great gift.

Week 10-Wednesday

Be Patient and Gentle with One Another

[1]As a prisoner for the Lord, then, I urge you to live a life worthy of the calling you have received. [2]Be completely humble and gentle; be patient, bearing with one another in love. [3]Make every effort to keep the unity of the Spirit through the bond of peace. [4]There is one body and one Spirit—just as you were called to one hope when you were called— [5]one Lord, one faith, one baptism; [6]one God and Father of all, who is over all and through all and in all. (Ephesians 4:1-6)

We know that judging others is wrong, but we do it anyway. However, we do not wish to be judged ourselves. We want to be accepted for who we are, yet, we cannot seem to accept others as they are. We want others to change, but we do not look at the things in our lives that need to be changed. We judge people by a single act, not realizing that there is so much more to the person than that they may do or say in one instance. If that is done to us, we feel that it is unfair. So, how do we stop judging others?

Be aware.

If you find yourself being judgmental, stop yourself. This takes a greater awareness than we usually have, so the first step (and an important one) is to observe your thoughts, trying to notice when you are being judgmental. This can be a difficult step. Remind yourself to observe.

Once you are more aware, you can then stop yourself when you feel yourself being judgmental.

Understand.

Instead of judging someone for what he has done or how he looks, try instead to understand the person. Put yourself in their shoes. Try to imagine their background. If possible, talk to them. Find out their story. Everyone has one. If not, try to imagine the circumstances that might have led to the person acting or looking like they do.

Accept.

Once you begin to understand, or at least think you understand, try to accept. Accept that person for who he is, without trying to change him. Accept that he will act the way he does, without wanting him to change. The world is what it is, and as much as you try, you can only change a little bit of it. It will continue to be as it is long after you are gone. Accept that, because otherwise, you are in for a world of frustration.

Love.

Once you have accepted someone for who he is, try to love him, even if you do not know him or even if you have hated him in the past. Love him as a brother, or love her as a sister, no matter who they are. What good will loving someone do? Your love will likely only be limited. However, it could have an effect on two people: yourself, and possibly, on the person for whom you have found love. Loving others will serve to make yourself happier. Trust me on this one. Loving others can change the lives of others, if you choose to express that love and take action on it. I cannot guarantee what will happen, but it can be life changing.

Week 10-Thursday

Blessed are you

[1]Now when he saw the crowds, he went up on a mountainside and sat down. His disciples came to him, [2]and he began to teach them saying:

[3]"Blessed are the poor in spirit,
for theirs is the kingdom of heaven.
[4]Blessed are those who mourn,
for they will be comforted.
[5]Blessed are the meek,
for they will inherit the earth.
[6]Blessed are those who hunger and thirst for righteousness,
for they will be filled.
[7]Blessed are the merciful,
for they will be shown mercy.
[8]Blessed are the pure in heart,
for they will see God.
[9]Blessed are the peacemakers,
for they will be called sons of God.
[10]Blessed are those who are persecuted because of righteousness,
for theirs is the kingdom of heaven.

[11]"Blessed are you when people insult you, persecute you, and falsely say all kinds of evil against you because of me. [12]Rejoice and be glad, because great is your reward in heaven, for in the same way they persecuted the prophets who were before you. (Matthew 5:1-12)

The message of Jesus was one of humility, charity, and brotherly love. He taught transformation of the inner person. Jesus presents the Beatitudes in a positive sense, virtues in life, which will ultimately lead to reward. Love becomes the motivation for the Christian. All of the Beatitudes have an eschatological meaning, that is, they promise us salvation, not in this world, but in the next. The Beatitudes initiate one of the main themes of Matthew's Gospel that the Kingdom so long awaited in the Old Testament is not of this world, but of the next, the Kingdom of Heaven.

Jesus describes those who are truly fortunate, the lucky ones of their day. However, it is not emperors, conquerors, priests, and the wealthy that enjoy this favor. Rather, it is the common people, those whom earthly success has largely passed by: the poor, the meek, the persecuted, and the peacemakers. How can this be? Because though they may have been denied worldly success, what cannot be taken away from them is their potential to live rightly by one another. It is all too easy for those who enjoy the pleasures of this world to try to float above such obligations.

Jesus goes on to say that so long as ordinary people stand for the right things and do not retreat in their rightness before those who seem to have more power, what is right will prevail. It is their kingdom—a kingdom organized not from the top down, but from the bottom up. In the Beatitudes, Jesus offers a description of the community of goodwill his teaching will build in this world.

While the Beatitudes of Jesus provide a way of life that promises salvation, they also provide peace in the midst of our trials and tribulations on this earth. The message contained within the Beatitudes can give us hope that the trials we face today will not last forever. There is a better life waiting for us if we do not lose faith in the God who loves us. The Kingdom of Heaven is ours.

Week 10-Friday

Jesus is our Living Hope

"3Praise be to the God and Father of our Lord Jesus Christ! In his great mercy he has given us new birth into a living hope through the resurrection of Jesus Christ from the dead, 4and into an inheritance that can never perish, spoil or fade—kept in heaven for you, 5who through faith are shielded by God's power until the coming of the salvation that is ready to be revealed in the last time. 6In this you greatly rejoice, though now for a little while you may have had to suffer grief in all kinds of trials. 7These have come so that your faith—of greater worth than gold, which perishes even though refined by fire—may be proved genuine and may result in praise, glory, and honor when Jesus Christ is revealed. 8Though you have not seen him, you love him; and even though you do not see him now, you believe in him and are filled with an inexpressible and glorious joy, 9for you are receiving the goal of your faith, the salvation of your souls". (1Peter 1:3-9)

The Christian life can be a glorious, hopeful existence even though the individual may face war, famine, illness, and other perils common to human existence. We do not, necessarily, hope for God to bless us with earthly riches, nor do we expect him to redeem his promises to us with earthly blessing. Our hope rests in the promise of an everlasting life near to God when Christ comes again. When under persecution, being put to death for their beliefs, Jesus' early followers died, gladly, a horrible and painful death, which they could have avoided by denying their Savior. They did so because they had seen and heard the Christ. They had seen His miracles, which proved him to be what he claimed himself to be, the Son of God. To them Jesus was the center of their hope. Time has not changed anything. Jesus is, today, the center of our hope, both in this life and forever after: Jesus is the Christ, the Son of God.

Week 10-Saturday

God's love removes all fear

"1When the day of Pentecost came, they were all together in one place. 2Suddenly a sound like the blowing of a violent wind came from heaven and filled the whole house where they were sitting. 3They saw what seemed to be tongues of fire that separated and came to rest on each of them. 4All of them were filled with the Holy Spirit and began to speak in other tongues as the Spirit enabled them.

5Now there were staying in Jerusalem God-fearing Jews from every nation under heaven. 6When they heard this sound, a crowd came together in bewilderment, because each one heard them speaking in his own language. 7Utterly amazed, they asked: "Are not all these men who are speaking Galileans? 8Then how is it that each of us hears them in his own native language? 9Parthians, Medes and Elamites; residents of Mesopotamia, Judea and Cappadocia, Pontus and Asia, 10Phrygia and Pamphylia, Egypt and the parts of Libya near Cyrene; visitors from Rome 11 (both Jews and converts to Judaism); Cretans and Arabs-we hear them declaring the wonders of God in our own tongues!" 12Amazed and perplexed, they asked one another, "What does this mean?"

13Some, however, made fun of them and said, "They have had too much wine."

14Then Peter stood up with the Eleven raised his voice and addressed the crowd: "Fellow Jews and all of you who live in Jerusalem, let me explain this to you; listen carefully to what I say. 15These men are not drunk, as you suppose. It is only nine in the morning! 16No, this is what was spoken by the prophet Joel:

17" 'In the last days, God says,
I will pour out my Spirit on all people.
Your sons and daughters will prophesy,
your young men will see visions,
your old men will dream dreams.
18Even on my servants, both men and women,

I will pour out my Spirit in those days,
and they will prophesy.
19I will show wonders in the heaven above
and signs on the earth below,
blood and fire and billows of smoke.
20The sun will be turned to darkness
and the moon to blood
before the coming of the great and glorious day of the Lord.
21And everyone who calls
on the name of the Lord will be saved.'

22"Men of Israel, listen to this: Jesus of Nazareth was a man accredited by God to you by miracles, wonders and signs, which God did among you through him, as you yourselves know. 23This man was handed over to you by God's set purpose and foreknowledge; and you, with the help of wicked men, put him to death by nailing him to the cross. 24But God raised him from the dead, freeing him from the agony of death, because it was impossible for death to keep its hold on him. 25David said about him:

"'I saw the Lord always before me. Because he is at my right hand,
I will not be shaken.
26Therefore my heart is glad and my tongue rejoices;
my body also will live in hope,
27because you will not abandon me to the grave,
nor will you let your Holy One see decay.
28You have made known to me the paths of life;
you will fill me with joy in your presence.' (Acts 2:1-28)

When we let, God take over our life we will start to live a life of love just as the disciples in the upper room did when they received the Holy Spirit on the day of Pentecost. If our heart is always open to love everyone then we keep our heart and life open for God to live in us. We cannot do the one without the other automatically happening. God is the Creator of love. God showed us perfect love by coming to die for us. God and love are bundled up in one package. If we have one, we will have the other.

Then, if we let God and love rule our lives, we have no reason to fear. We have no reason to fear judgment and we have no reason to fear anyone else. It does not matter what anyone might do, we are safely tucked in the arms of God, and we know that whatever happens, we will one day be in Heaven. These bodies we have are just temporary bodies. We will have new ones in Heaven. This earth, as it is now, is only temporary. There is nothing on this earth worth hanging on to and worrying over. It will all be burned up and wiped away in the end and a new earth will be in its place. The minute fear and worry hits, the first thing a person needs to do is start praying. If someone is causing us to worry, that is the time to pray for help to see them the way God sees them and to love them as God loves them.

If we say we love God and then retaliate or seek revenge against someone, we are a liar. That is not just my words. The Bible says it. We cannot hate another or strike out at another if we love God. When we love someone, we do not want to do anything that would hurt them. When we hate someone, we are hating someone that God dearly loves, and we are disappointing God with our actions. Notice the Bible also points out that if we cannot love someone we can see, how can we love someone we cannot see? Therefore, if we cannot show love to those around us that we can see, then we do not have the kind of love that can love someone we cannot see. Love and God come in one package. We cannot have one and not have the other.

Week 10-Sunday

No one can separate us from God

"31What, then, shall we say in response to this? If God is for us, who can be against us? 32He who did not spare his own Son, but gave him up for us all—how will he not also, along with him, graciously give us all things? 33Who will bring any charge against those whom God has chosen. God justifies. 34Who is he that condemns? Christ Jesus, who died—more than that, who was raised to life—is at the right hand of God and is also interceding for us. 35Who shall separate us from the love of Christ? Shall trouble or hardship or persecution or famine or nakedness or danger or sword? 36As it is written:

"For your sake we face death all day long;

we are considered as sheep to be slaughtered." 37No, in all these things we are more than conquerors through him who loved us. 38For I am convinced that neither death nor life, neither angels nor demons, either the present nor the future, nor any powers, 39neither height nor depth, nor anything else in all creation, will be able to separate us from the love of God that is in Christ Jesus our Lord." (Romans 8:31-39)

This passage encourages and comforts us pointing out that no matter what situations we face, none of them can separate us from the love that God has towards us. In addition, no one, including people and evil spirits, can take us away from the love of God. This is very important for us to know and believe, especially when things seem to be difficult or impossible for us to manage, when the way ahead appears to be very dark, when we do not know which way to turn or to whom to turn to.

We need to remember at such times that even though God has allowed us to face such situations, His love for us has not changed a bit. He has permitted such things to happen to us because He knows that we should be able to bear them with the help of His grace. If we love God, God will cause all these things to work together for our good. Trust in God's love and know that no matter what is happening to you, you do not face these things alone. God is always with us.

Week 11-Monday

Jesus Forgives our Failings

15When they had finished eating, Jesus said to Simon Peter, "Simon son of John, do you truly love me more than these?"

"Yes, Lord," he said, "you know that I love you."

Jesus said, "Feed my lambs."

16Again Jesus said, "Simon son of John, do you truly love me?"

He answered, "Yes, Lord, you know that I love you."

Jesus said, "Take care of my sheep."

17 The third time he said to him, "Simon son of John, do you love me?"

Peter was hurt because Jesus asked him the third time, "Do you love me?" He said, "Lord, you know all things; you know that I love you."

Jesus said, "Feed my sheep.

18 I tell you the truth, when you were younger you dressed yourself and went where you wanted; but when you are old you will stretch out your hands, and someone else will dress you and lead you where you do not want to go." 19Jesus said this to indicate the kind of death by which Peter would glorify God. Then he said to him, "Follow me!" (John 21:15-19)

In this discourse, Jesus forgives Peter. You would not expect Jesus to even consider Peter for the important job of looking after the flock. However, Jesus could see his heart and knew he was the man for the job. Why? Peter grew through his mistake. Peter reformed himself after his mistake. Peter knew what it was to be human, and Peter grew to accept himself and his humanity and move on from his sinfulness. Three times Peter had denied Jesus by a fire on Holy Thursday evening but now three times by a different fire on this Easter day Jesus asks Peter to look after the sheep. Jesus forgave Peter and had confidence in him to make him "the Rock" of his church.

Despite our sinfulness, Jesus forgives us and has confidence in us. In the second letter to Timothy we read, "We may be unfaithful, but he is always faithful, for he cannot deny his own self" (2 Tim 2:13). Jesus does not lock us in by mistakes of the past or present. We are given room to outgrow the mistakes of the past. Paul wrote, "for anyone who is in Christ, there is a new creation; the old creation has gone, and now the new one is here."

If we find it difficult to accept ourselves with our faults and failings, then it is no wonder we find it difficult to believe that God can forgive our faults and failings. What happened to Peter can happen to us also if we have the faith to accept God's love and acceptance of us. Jesus forgives us and accepts us after we have denied him, after we have disbelieved, after we have given up, after we have sinned. It takes an act of faith to believe in God, and it takes an act of faith to believe that God forgives us and accepts our repentance and us after sin. Sometimes faith is the courage to accept acceptance, the courage to accept God's forgiveness and acceptance of ourselves. Peter recovered his faith after his despair; he was able to say, "Yes Lord, you know that I love you."

So let us not allow the past to overcome us. Instead, let us be like Peter, repent, reform ourselves, and allow the Lord to put us to work for him again,

Week 11-Tuesday

Care about others

"This is how we know what love is: Jesus Christ laid down his life for us. And we ought to lay down our lives for our brothers. If anyone has material possessions and sees his brother in need but has no pity on him, how can the love of God be in him? Dear children, let us not love with words or tongue but with actions and in truth. This then is how we know that we belong to the truth, and how we set our hearts at rest in his presence whenever our hearts condemn us. For God is greater than our hearts, and he knows everything" (1 John 3: 16-20).

You will never find peace by being self-consumed and only worrying about your own needs and wants. When you begin to genuinely care about other people, so much goodness comes right out. This only helps into solidifying your inner peace. It can be people close to you or pure strangers, but any act of kindness and goodwill eases your way towards peace and closer to Jesus. When I help other people, I stop focusing on my so-called problems and realize that my life is not so bad after all. This rids my entire being of all the stress and feelings of being overwhelmed. There is great peace and wisdom in thinking and caring about other people, which we are blind to when we are too deep within our own selfish ways.

Week 11-Wednesday

God does not cause Bad Things to Happen to Good People

28"Come to me, all you who are weary and burdened, and I will give you rest. 29Take my yoke upon you and learn from me, for I am gentle and humble in heart, and you will find rest for your souls. 30For my yoke is easy and my burden is light." (Matthew 11:28-30)

It is sad to listen to people say that "God is testing me," "God is punishing me for something that I did wrong", "I want to keep God happy so he won't cause bad things to happen to me".

God does not make bad things happen. God is not looking to find fault with you. God is looking to encourage the best in you. God wants you to be the person you were born to be. God is not a punishing, wrathful, or angry God.

I think that if God were that way, he would have zapped us into oblivion a long time ago. The God I know and love is loving, caring, compassionate, forgiving, generous, and very patient. The punishing God that we may have heard about in our childhood does not exist. I know that is hard for some to believe, but it is true. God does not test us; he knows how weak we are already. God does not give us us bad things, we can find those very easily on our own. Remember, there is Satan who would like us to blame God and turn away from God. Think of what Jesus did for us and gave up for us. Is that the sign of a vengeful, punishing God? I do not think so.

Therefore, as you go through your day, if bad things do happen, ask God to help you. Stop and talk to him right then and there. I guarantee that you will not be disappointed.

Week 11-Thursday

There is no room for prejudice in the Kingdom of Jesus.

"My brothers, as believers in our glorious Lord Jesus Christ, don't show favoritism. Suppose a man comes into your meeting wearing a gold ring and fine clothes, and a poor man in shabby clothes also comes in. If you show special attention to the man wearing fine clothes and say, "Here's a good seat for you," but say to the poor man, "You stand there" or "Sit on the floor by my feet," have you not discriminated among yourselves and become judges with evil thoughts?

Listen, my dear brothers: Has not God chosen those who are poor in the eyes of the world to be rich in faith and to inherit the kingdom he promised those who love him? But you have insulted the poor. Is it not the rich who are exploiting you? Are they not the ones who are dragging you into court? Are they not the ones who are slandering the noble name of him to whom you belong?

If you really keep the royal law found in Scripture, "Love your neighbor as yourself, "you are doing right. But if you show favoritism, you sin and are convicted by the law as lawbreakers" (James 2:1-9).

This past Week I was witness to discrimination. A Catholic school denied entry to a child whose parents were lesbians. One of the arguments given by the school is that they were following the teachings of Jesus.

Did Jesus Ever Condemn Homosexuality?

There is no New Testament record of where Jesus explicitly stated that homosexuality is wrong. If you believe that homosexuality is something you are born with, not a life choice, then you cannot assume that Jesus would have condemned it. There are many difference we recognize in each other as being OK; eye color, hair color, skin color, height, weight, smart, not-smart, just to name a few. Then why would a difference in sexual orientation cause such a problem for people.

If your are prejudice against homosexuality, own it, do not try to blame it on Jesus.

Jesus had love for all. He did not discriminate against any group. In fact, Jesus sought out those people who needed love, because no one else loved them. So, do not attribute to Jesus the characteristic of prejudice that belongs to us. We discriminate, we are prejudice, we hate, and we have little tolerance. We must own this, but that does not mean that we should not work to change these destructive traits in our character.

I encourage all who wish to be good disciples of Jesus, to read the entire letter of James in the Bible. James tells it like it is. Further, I do not think that it was the intention of the people who put together the Scriptures, that it be used to hurt people. That could not possibly be Jesus' teachings. He came to heal us, not to condemn us. If you read the four Gospels, you will find that Jesus only took issue with the Scribes and Pharisees because of their judging and condemning ways. They were hurting his people, not loving them.

The teachings of Jesus are loving, kind, compassionate, tolerant, and forgiving. Those who try to use his teachings to condemn people just do not get it. Do not let it be you!

Week 11-Friday

The Scriptures are not a weapon

30 "Give to everyone who asks you. And if anyone takes what belongs to you, do not ask to get it back. 31 Do to others, as you want them to do to you. 32 "Suppose you love those who love you. Should anyone praise you for that? Even 'sinners' love those who love them. 33 And suppose you do good to those who are good to you. Should anyone praise you for that? Even 'sinners' do that. 34 And suppose you lend money to those who can pay you back. Should anyone praise you for that? Even a 'sinner' lends to 'sinners,' expecting them to pay everything back.

35 "But love your enemies. Do good to them. Lend to them without expecting to get anything back. Then you will receive a lot in return. And you will be sons of the Most High God. He is kind to people who are evil and are not thankful. 36 So, have mercy, just as your Father has mercy.

37 "If you do not judge others, then you will not be judged. If you do not find others guilty, then you will not be found guilty. Forgive, and you will be forgiven. 38 Give and it will be given to you. A good amount will be poured into your lap. It will be pressed down, shaken together, and running over. The same amount you give will be measured out to you." (Luke 6:30-38)

I was recently witness to a situation where someone was injured; not physically, but emotionally. The person doing the hurt said that they were showing "tough love." This was done because someone was seen to have broken a rule of the Church. Even though I believe that sometimes tough love is necessary, it did not seem appropriate to me in this case. A single verse was taken from Scriptures and used as justification for the injury.

I do not believe that the Scriptures are to be used to hurt people. When we take a line or passage of the Scriptures out of its context, and use it as a weapon, it is us who have committed a sin against God and also a sin against our brothers and sisters in God.

When Jesus quoted the Old Testament, it was always for a positive purpose. He did not do this to hurt people, but instead to help people, who were themselves being persecuted by the religious leaders.

The message I get from Jesus is that it is never wrong to be merciful to others. It is never right to judge others. Those who tell you otherwise, do not understand the message of Jesus. If you believe that the Scriptures are the word of God, then the message must be positive. If we use Scriptures as examples, we must be careful to avoid beating someone with them. The Scriptures should be used to encourage not to discourage. The message of Jesus was one of love.

In the words of St. Paul:

"Love is patient, love is kind. It is not jealous, (love) is not pompous, it is not inflated, it is not rude, it does not seek its own interests, it is not quick-tempered, it does not brood over injury, and it does not rejoice over wrongdoing but rejoices with the truth. It bears all things, believes all things, hopes all things, and endures all things. Love never fails." (1 Cor 13: 3-4)

Use the Scriptures to show love, not as a justification for injuring or judging others.

Week 11-Saturday

Accept what is, yet do what you can do!

6 "Aren't five sparrows sold for two pennies? But God does not forget even one of them. 7 In fact, he even counts every hair on your head! So do not be afraid. You are worth more than many sparrows." (Luke 12:6-7)

In the above passage, Jesus is trying to tell the people that God will be there for them, if they would only have trust. Still, it is a common human condition to worry. However, there is only so much we can affect. What we cannot change, what we cannot influence no matter what, should not be a concern to us. This is what I notice with so many people, in that we focus and linger on things, which we have no control over.

Why worry about something that not all the worrying in the world will change? Why care about what other people think of us when we are not even sure what it is they are actually thinking? Once you open the blinds to this fact, and start accepting what is that you cannot change, you automatically relieve yourself of a mountain of stress and anxiety. It is like a huge weight has been lifted from your shoulders. Taking this path is following a road towards peace. Give up your trouble, worry, and anxiety to God. However, do not try to take it back when it appears that God is not moving fast enough.

I think that when you have an opportunity to affect change, you should take that opportunity. You should speak out against wrongdoing. Do help those that are put in your path to help.

That may seem to contradict what I wrote about worrying. That is the difference between worrying and doing. Do what you can and let God take care of the rest.

Week 11-Sunday

Love is Always the Answer

"8 Pay everything you owe. But you can never pay back all the love you owe each other. Those who love others have done everything the law requires. 9 Here are some commandments to think about. "Do not commit adultery." "Do not commit murder." "Do not steal." "Do not want what belongs to others."—(Exodus 20:13-15, 17; Deuteronomy 5:17-19, 21) These and other commandments are all included in one rule. Here is what it is. "Love your neighbor as you love yourself."—(Leviticus 19:18) 10 Love does not harm its neighbor. So love does everything the law requires." (Romans 13:8-10)

If you truly love someone, you will do great acts, put up with hurt, forgive injuries, and act with kindness and compassion. This is Jesus' message. Everything we do should be done with love. We sometimes forget how interconnected we are and how much we need one another. We were given different gifts so that we must work together in harmony.

If you have the gift of writing, always write what is good. If you have the gift of speaking, let nothing come out of your mouth but the truth, said with love. If you are an artist, paint the good of the world. If you are an artisan, create only what is good. Go through your day with happiness and a grateful heart. If we who know Jesus can do these little things to follow his teachings, we can help to transform the world.

It is never wrong to act out of love and compassion; do not let anyone tell you differently. Love is always the answer

Week 12-Monday

Focus on Christ

"10 Brothers and sisters, I ask all of you to agree with one another. I make my appeal in the name of our Lord Jesus Christ. Then you will not take sides. You will be in complete agreement in all that you think.

11 My brothers and sisters, some people who live in Chloe's house have told me you are arguing with each other. 12 Here is what I mean. One of you says, "I follow Paul." Another says, "I follow Apollos." Another says, "I follow Peter." And still another says, "I follow Christ."

13 Does Christ take sides? Did Paul die on the cross for you? Were you baptized in the name of Paul? 14 I am thankful that I did not baptize any of you except Crispus and Gaius. 15 No one can say that you were baptized in my name.

16 It is true that I also baptized those who live in the house of Stephanas. Besides that, I do not remember if I baptized anyone else.

17 Christ did not send me to baptize. He sent me to preach the good news. He commanded me not to use the kind of wisdom that people commonly use. That would take all the power away from the cross of Christ" (1Cor 1:10-17).

Even though the above passage in Paul refers to a specific group of the house church of Chloe, it is very timely for us as well. Our focus should not be in the specific Christian denomination to which we belong. Our focus should always be Christ. We do not worship the Church, or at least we should not, we worship Christ.

I believe that our denominations are merely a language that facilitates our coming together. I may speak Catholic; whereas you may speak Lutheran; someone else may speak Baptist. It does not matter what language we use to praise and give glory to God in community, what matters is that we do it. It would be nice if we all spoke the same language, but being that we are all different, we speak to God in different ways. It is important for us to come together as a community focused on Christ. It is important for us to share in the praise of the God who loves us.

There is no Christian denomination that is the correct one; all the Christian languages have flaws. If we really focus on Christ, it does not matter how we do it. If we truly focus on Christ and become his followers, it is easy to accept the differences of others. We should come to our churches with the object of developing fellowship and love for one another. In focusing on Christ, the differences melt away, for we are all one in Christ.

Week 12-Tuesday

The New Covenant—Jesus Christ

"I will keep you and will make you to be a covenant for the people and a light for the Gentiles (Isaiah 42:6; 49:8).

This cup is the new covenant in my blood, which is poured out for you (Luke 22:20)."

"As for me, this is my covenant with them, says the LORD. My Spirit, who is on you, and my words that I have put in your mouth will not depart from your mouth, or from the mouths of your children, or from the mouths of their descendants from this time on and forever, says the LORD." (Isaiah 59:21)

The connection between Jesus Christ and the new covenant is made explicit in the passage that began: *"This cup is the new covenant in my blood. Do this as often as you drink it in remembrance of me" (1 Corinthians 11.25).*

The mention of a covenant ratified by his blood recalls the covenant that is sealed by blood in Exodus 24.6-8, and identifies Jesus' death as an act of covenant renewal (cf. Is 53.12, "He poured out his soul to death…yet he bore the sin of many"; and Zech 9.11, where the liberation of prisoners is made possible by "the blood of the covenant"). Jesus gives his life for the forfeited life of others. The forgiveness and liberation promised in Jeremiah 31.31 ff. as marks of the new covenant are thereby realized in Jesus: "This cup, poured out for you, is the new covenant sealed by my blood" (Mk 14.24; Lk 22.29).

Through Christ's life, death and resurrection God inaugurates and seals with (God's!) blood the new covenant, which ensures the forgiveness of all sins, secures the final victory over every form of death, and guarantees the coming end-time when all humanity will be reconciled with God, with each other and with creation, and "Christ is all and in all" (Col 3.11).

The Lord's Supper is more than a service to remember the person and work of Jesus. Rather, it is an empowering sacrament through which the promise of the real presence of Jesus and his gift of forgiveness are given and sealed as we partake of the bread and cup. Like covenant, therefore, the sacrament is a profound transforming power. However, the sacrament is even more than that. It is also profound in that through the bread and cup Jesus Christ empowers and calls the covenant community (church) to his work of justice, peace and a renewed creation against the powers of this present Dark Age (Eph 6.12).

It is we who benefit from this covenant. Christ did not just come for the people of his own time. He came for all of us here and now. Jesus is the Law of God inscribed in our hearts by The Holy Spirit and so he is the stone the builders rejected (Matt 21:42). Though Moses gave them Ten Commandments, Jesus gave us just two commandments, to love God and to love one another. Sometimes we tend to forget that second commandment. "As I have loved you, so you must love one another (John 13:34; 15:12, 17)". This commandment we are to receive by faith, knowing that he watches over his word to perform it, and so we fulfill the whole Law and thereby we must be the fruit of that love, by being love for God and for all that God loves. Love knows all the pressing needs in God's house and Love also knows the neighbor down the street who just lost his job. Jesus Christ is everything in this glorious New Covenant: "I will keep you and will make you to be a covenant for the people and a light for the Gentiles (Isaiah 42:6; 49:8).

Week 12-Wednesday

We know what love is.

"We know what love is because Jesus Christ gave his life for us. So we should give our lives for our brothers and sisters." (1 John 3:16)

A PRAYER FOR LOVE

Teach me to love, Jesus, as you love,
Make it unconditional, honest, and kind,
to ask nothing back in return, Jesus,
to encompass the whole of humankind.

May I offer my love without speaking,
May it radiate as it shines forth from me,
May it be seen in my face and my eyes, Jesus,
May it be simple, sincere, and shame free.

Show me how to forgive, Jesus, as You do,
To not burden another with guilt,
To not play the role of the martyr,
To be a rock on which trust may be built.

Make my love for others be greater by far
than any love that is offered to me,
Led by the Spirit, Inspired of God,
As forgiving as Jesus, and free.

I hope that you find it in your heart to love today.

Week 12-Thursday

God Gives Comfort

"3 Give praise to the God and Father of our Lord Jesus Christ! He is the Father who gives tender love. All comfort comes from him. 4 He comforts us in all our troubles. Now we can comfort others when they are in trouble. We ourselves have received comfort from God. 5 We share the sufferings of Christ. We also share his comfort" (2 Corinthians 1:3-5).

As humans, comfort and security are two of our greatest needs. They are as strong the need for food or warmth. I think we have all experienced times when we were so anxious about something that we could not think of food. Children are very open about their fears. They are often more easily comforted. As children, a snuggle with mommy and daddy, or a cup of warm milk, was often enough to calm our fears. A good teddy bear and a warm blanket would make the night seem friendlier.

However, as we get older, the fears grow greater, the night seems darker and somehow, our teddy bears seem smaller. It is not enough to have a fuzzy little body to hold. Sometimes we try to fill that gap by looking for a larger body to hold. We look to marriage as our defense against our fears. However, no one man or woman can provide complete security. There are too many worries, too much heartbreak out there for the best of husbands or wives, the best of teddy bears.

God knows how desperately we need to be comforted. The Scriptures are full of references to sorrow, fears, loneliness, and the comfort God provides. When Christ told the disciples of his impending death, he knew that they would need comforting more at this time of their lives than at any other. In addition, he knew they would need strength to persevere through the difficulties ahead. Therefore, he gave the assurance of the Comforter, the Holy Spirit.

The wonderful thing is, those same promises apply to us. We also have access to that comforter. He is ever present, and understands our every need. John 14:27 says, "*Peace I leave with you; my peace I give to you; not as the world gives do I give to you. Let not your hearts be troubled, neither let them be afraid.*" Therefore, we know that we can rely on God to listen to our fears and give us comfort.

His Word is also a great source of comfort. How many of us have turned to the Psalms to reassure us in times of trouble. The 23rd Psalm is probably the most frequently quoted piece of literature at funerals, because this image of God as our Shepherd is so comforting, even to those who do not have a personal relationship with Him. In Psalm 119:28 David says, *"My soul is weary with sorrow; strengthen me according to your word."*

God has left His written word for us as a tool for instruction and comfort. When we immerse ourselves in the Scriptures daily, those passages will come back to us in times of trouble. We should not be afraid to seek God when we experience trouble and heartache, and need comfort. God is waiting for us his children to recognize that he is there. He wants to help us through these troubled times in our lives. God is never too busy to listen to us and to comfort us.

Week 12-Friday

Do you talk about God or do you talk to God?

"I have much more to say to you, more than you can now bear. But when he, the Spirit of truth, comes, he will guide you into all truth. He will not speak on his own; he will speak only what he hears, and he will tell you what is yet to come. He will bring glory to me by taking from what is mine and making it known to you. All that belongs to the Father is mine. That is why I said the Spirit will take from what is mine and make it known to you." (John 16:12-15)

Spiritual direction (also known as spiritual guidance, spiritual friendship, or spiritual companionship) starts with a desire to live a life more centered in God and the knowledge that help and guidance are needed to do so. The person desiring direction (often called the "directee") seeks another individual to help guide, support, and listen together for God. The purpose of spiritual direction is to help people become aware of the mystery of God's presence and action in human experience, and to assist them in making fuller and freer response to it.

Spiritual direction is the ancient practice of spiritual friendship and mentoring in which one spiritual seeker joins another on his or her spiritual journey, giving counsel and encouragement along the way. It is a discipline practiced in many religions and cultural traditions including shamanism, Christian mysticism, Islamic Sufi practice, and Hindu Gurus. All are considered to be valid attempts to follow a path which leads to a deep experience of God's transcendent presence.

Basically, it is up to both the director and directee to listen for the voice of Spirit as the stories of one's life are related, grounding them in scripture, theology and tradition while still being open to the new thing that God may wish to bring forth. The difference here is that we are not just talking about God but relating details of our personal experience of and relationship with God.

Therefore, spiritual direction avoids the realm of talk about God, which often enters into discussions of theology, belief systems, dogma, and tradition. Spiritual direction is about entering into a relationship of sharing deeply one's actual experiences of God for the purpose of learning more about ourselves and the desires of the one who created us as we are.

As such, this daring adventure that cannot be entered into without significant investment of one's self and a willingness to reveal what lies at the depths of one's soul. The rewards are great but the risk is ultimate in that one who truly desires to know God and to be completely open to God can hold nothing back in the end. Of course, no one starts out at such a level of complete openness and honesty and often much time is required in order to reach the point of being so vulnerable and so completely transparent. This level of transparency can only happen when one comes to know the sheer depth of God's grace and when one understands the cross as a measure of the willingness of God to do whatever it takes to be in relationship with us.

The advantage of spiritual direction is that trained directors can often observe things about the way you tell your story that remain hidden to you. These little revelations are often the keys to opening up deep, hidden pockets of self-knowledge and ways of being with God that would otherwise remain obscured. If you sincerely desire to know God more intimately, spiritual direction may be worth considering as a way of getting beyond your own limits of understanding God and becoming open to the ways God seeks to be present in your life.

Week 12-Saturday

Wisdom

"But the wisdom that comes from heaven is first of all pure; then peace-loving, considerate, submissive, full of mercy and good fruit, impartial and sincere. Peacemakers who sow in peace raise a harvest of righteousness." (James 3:17-18)

Who are the wise among us today? What you are doing right now is the wisest thing you can possibly do. You are worshiping God. You are making God the center of your life. You are falling at the feet of Jesus to hear his word.

You can study many things and be a great scholar, and know everything about the earth and the sky, but if you do not know Jesus, you have missed what is good and true about our world. With Jesus to guide us, we have peace and love to help us cope with the problems of this world. We have Jesus to watch over us and protect us. With Jesus, we can find rest for our souls.

Get to know Jesus.

Week 12-Sunday

Do you have a Spiritual Practice?

"The Spirit gives life; the flesh counts for nothing. The words I have spoken to you are spirit and they are life. Yet there are some of you who do not believe." For Jesus had known from the beginning which of them did not believe and who would betray him" (John 6:63-64).

How do you feed the Spirit within You?

Each of us has our reasons for wanting to start this spiritual journey. Perhaps you have experienced some kind of awakening and know that your life will never be the same. If you were raised in the Christian faith, you may have come to a point when you want to dip into the spiritual river that flows through all the traditions. However, most of us, frankly, are drawn to spirituality because, as a doctor might say, certain symptoms are "presenting."

You might feel that something is missing in your life, something you desperately want. You could be longing for inspiration. Or community. Or quality time. You could be in pain and in need of healing. You could be feeling happy and grateful and compelled to give something back to God. You could be facing a crisis and know that how you handled such situations in the past will not be enough this time. You could be burned out. You could be worried about your loved ones or frightened about the very real dangers in the world. You could be sensing that your life could be more meaningful but not know how to go about making it so.

Take heart! These real-life feelings, challenges, and experiences are just what spiritual practices are for. Defined simply, spiritual practices are activities we do to move into deeper relationships with God.

God continually tries to draw us into relationship with himself, but we may not listen to God unless we experience a life-changing event and know we cannot handle it on our own. God then picks us up, welcomes us, and helps us to walk with him on a road of his choosing. The road we are meant to travel. "Be not afraid"!

Week 13-Wednesday

Getting to Know Jesus.

"He who says, "I know Him," and does not keep His commandments, is a liar, and the truth is not in him" (1 John 2:4).

Jesus should be the inspiration of every life in every generation. However, many people do not know or understand what Jesus was all about. He was not about power, not about money, not about condemnation, not about unworthiness. Jesus came to show us how to live and how to love. He came to make our lives easier. Society creates many complex rules and regulations both written and unwritten. Society will give you the parameters to understand who is good and who is bad, who is right and who is wrong, who is important and who is not. Unfortunately, these are changing targets. Depending upon whom you are talking to, these measures can change.

With Jesus, everyone has potential to be good, you are right if you follow his example on living, and everyone is important and significant in the eyes of God. Jesus' simple rule is one of love, which does not change with the times, your economic status, your education level, or your place in society. With Jesus, all are equal, all are worthy, all are loved, and all are forgiven.

We make life complicated. Jesus came to make our lives easier. He came to take away the pressures of how to live, how to fit into society, and how to treat one another. The simple rule is love. It is not merely a romantic love; it is a choice we make. If we understand the message of Jesus, we know that love is patient, forgiving, compassionate, and understanding. It is caring for one another. It is noticing the needs of one another. It is being present to everyone in a loving, caring way.

If you truly know Jesus, you cannot help but follow his example. If you do not know Jesus, learn about him. Look at his life. Look at how he treated people. Look at how he made everyone feel loved, especially those who were deemed unlovable by society. He helped those who society had abandoned. His manner was truly inspirational.

Week 13-Monday

Journey to Christ

"These people honor me with their lips,
but their hearts are far from me.
They worship me in vain;
their teachings are but rules taught by men." (Matthew 15:8-9)

When I choose Jesus, I began to make changes in my life. At first, the choice of living Jesus was not outwardly apparent because I was struggling interiorly—that is, I was striving to conform myself to live like Jesus. Only after some progress has been made interiorly will an outward difference be visible…At first, it was not apparent because I was working on myself—on striving to recognize and fix my own problems and imperfections through the means of prayer and my interior relationship with Christ. Eventually, an outward sign became visible. I begin to be more patient, and more pleasant to other. I did things for others without complaint.

Outwardly, I still do the same job every day, but now I do it with and for Jesus. The job is the same, but now it is pleasing to God. Others soon noticed that I possess some new interior joy or happiness that originally was not there. This new joy comes from my choosing Jesus. I chose Christ and allowed Him to take possession of me, and through the relationship we now share, I now live life in a different manner and style.

I am not trying to say that I am always doing it perfectly, far from it. I have to struggle every day with my weaknesses. However, I live my life joyfully; being aware of all the blessings, God has given to gifts and me to help me to help others. My life is becoming a life of love. It is not a life of rules made by man. It is a life of kindness, compassion, forgiveness, and peace fashioned by Jesus. It is a gift I want to share with others.

Week 13-Tuesday

Do not fear, God is always with us.

14"Again, it will be like a man going on a journey, who called his servants and entrusted his property to them. 15To one he gave five talents[a] of money, to another two talents, and to another one talent, each according to his ability. Then he went on his journey. 16The man who had received the five talents went at once, put his money to work, and gained five more. 17So also, the one with the two talents gained two more. 18But the man who had received the one talent went off dug a hole in the ground and hid his master's money.

19"After a long time the master of those servants returned and settled accounts with them. 20The man who had received the five talents brought the other five. 'Master,' he said, 'you entrusted me with five talents. See, I have gained five more.'

21"His master replied, 'Well done, good, and faithful servant! You have been faithful with a few things; I will put you in charge of many things. Come and share your master's happiness!'

22"The man with the two talents also came. 'Master,' he said, 'you entrusted me with two talents; see, I have gained two more.'

23"His master replied, 'well done, good, and faithful servant! You have been faithful with a few things; I will put you in charge of many things. Come and share your master's happiness!'

24"Then the man who had received the one talent came. 'Master,' he said, 'I knew that you are a hard man, harvesting where you have not sown and gathering where you have not scattered seed. 25So I was afraid and went out and hid your talent in the ground. See, here is what belongs to you.'

26"His master replied, 'you wicked, lazy servant! So you knew that I harvest where I have not sown and gather where I have not scattered seed. 27Well then, you should have put my money on deposit with the bankers, so that when I returned I would have received it back with interest.

28" 'Take the talent from him and give it to the one who has the talents. 29For everyone who has will be given more, and he will h an abundance. Whoever does not have, even what he has will be ta from him. 30And throw that worthless servant outside, into darkness, where there will be weeping and gnashing teeth"(Matthew 25:14-30).

How many of us are afraid to use the talents that God has give God gives us these talents so that we may help one another. The useless if we hide them or keep them only to ourselves.

It is often fear that causes us to hide our talents instead of them. Lack of use often causes decay. Therefore, the talents we given are lost if they are not used.

As in the parable above, we must put our talents to good use in to develop them to the fullest. The fear of failure must be overco order for us to reach our full potential. God is there to help us alo way and will be there to help us get up when we may fall. We ne fear that we are all alone. God is always there.

Week 13-Thursday

Do not judge or you will be judged in the same manner.

"Do not judge or you too will be judged. For in the same way you judge others, you will be judged, and with the measure you use, it will be measured to you.

"Why do you look at the speck of sawdust in your brother's eye and pay no attention to the plank in your own eye? How can you say to your brother, 'Let me take the speck out of your eye,' when all the time there is a plank in your own eye? You hypocrite, first take the plank out of your own eye, and then you will see clearly to remove the speck from your brother's eye" (Matthew 7:1-5).

Judge not, that you be not judged: With this command, Jesus warned against passing judgment upon others, because when we do so we will be judged in a similar manner.

Most people who quote this verse do not understand what Jesus said. They seem to think (or hope) that Jesus commanded a universal acceptance of any lifestyle or teaching. There are things that can never be considered acceptable, but before we criticize others, we must make sure that we are not doing those things ourselves.

So while this does not completely prohibit examining the lives of others, it certainly prohibits doing in the spirit it is often done. An example of unjust judgment was the disciples' condemnation of the woman who came to anoint the feet of Jesus with oil (Matthew 26:6-13). They thought she was wasting something; Jesus said she had done a good thing that would always be remembered. They had a rash, harsh, unjust judgment of her.

1. We break this command when we think the worst of others.
2. We break this command when we only speak to others of their faults.
3. We break this command when we judge an entire life only by its worst moments.

4. We break this command when we judge the hidden motives of others.

5. We break this command when we judge others without considering ourselves in their same circumstances.

6. We break this command when we judge others without being mindful that we ourselves will be judged.

When our judgment about others is wrong, it is often not because we judge according to a standard but because we are hypocritical in the application of that standard. We ignore the standard in our own life. It is common to judge others by one standard and ourselves by another standard, being far more generous to ourselves than others are.

Why do you look at the speck of sawdust in your brother's eye, but do not consider the plank in your own eye? The figures of a speck and a plank are real figures, yet used humorously. Jesus shows how we are generally far more tolerant to our own sin than we are to the sin of others.

Jesus is gentle, but he calls a person a 'hypocrite' who fusses about small things in others, and pays no attention to great matters at home in his/her own person.

Jesus did not say that it was wrong for us to help others with the specks in their eyes. It is a good thing to help others, but not before dealing with our own very large issues.

I hope that Jesus will be kinder to me when it comes time to look back at the issues of my live, than I have often been in dealing with others.

Week 13-Friday

The Beatitudes are Gifts of the Spirit

The Beatitudes

"1Now when he saw the crowds, he went up on a mountainside and sat down. His disciples came to him, 2and he began to teach them saying:

3"Blessed are the poor in spirit,
for theirs is the kingdom of heaven.
4Blessed are those who mourn,
for they will be comforted.
5Blessed are the meek,
for they will inherit the earth.
6Blessed are those who hunger and thirst for righteousness,
for they will be filled.
7Blessed are the merciful,
for they will be shown mercy.
8Blessed are the pure in heart,
for they will see God.
9Blessed are the peacemakers,
for they will be called sons of God.
10Blessed are those who are persecuted because of righteousness,
for theirs is the kingdom of heaven.

11"Blessed are you when people insult you, persecute you, and falsely say all kinds of evil against you because of me. 12Rejoice and be glad, because great is your reward in heaven, for in the same way they persecuted the prophets who were before you"(Matthew 5:1-12).

The Sermon on the Mount is the "charter" to ethical living for all Christians. It is not just a list of different groups; it is a ladder, which will bring one on the path to following Jesus. We will go through on our way to the "Kingdom of God" a process. The Holy Spirit inspires each step. The following is one interpretation of this ladder:

Blessed are those who have emptied themselves and realize that they are nothing without God.

Blessed are those who are sorry for all the sins they have committed against God and neighbor.

Blessed are those who are open to the movement of the Spirit within their lives.

Blessed are those who seek justice for all those who are forgotten by society.

Blessed are those who practice love, compassion, faithfulness, and forgiveness to all.

Blessed are those whose intention is pure and are not seekers of fame.

Blessed are those who externally express peace both verbally and non-verbally.

Blessed are those who know that they are on a road that will take them to their own cross.

Blessed are those who will suffer and are ridiculed because of their love and faith in Jesus.

For them, the "Kingdom of Heaven" is at hand.

Week 13-Saturday

The Day and Hour of the End is Unknown

36"No one knows about that day or hour, not even the angels in heaven, nor the Son, but only the Father. 37As it was in the days of Noah, so it will be at the coming of the Son of Man. 38For in the days before the flood, people were eating and drinking, marrying and giving in marriage, up to the day Noah entered the ark; 39and they knew nothing about what would happen until the flood came and took them all away. That is how it will be at the coming of the Son of Man. 40Two men will be in the field; one will be taken and the other left. 41Two women will be grinding with a hand mill; one will be taken and the other left.

42"Therefore keep watch, because you do not know on what day your Lord will come. 43But understand this: If the owner of the house had known at what time of night the thief was coming, he would have kept watch and would not have let his house be broken into. 44So you also must be ready, because the Son of Man will come at an hour when you do not expect him." (Matthew 24:36-44)

Many people are saying that in 2012, the world will end. They even made a movie about it. I also remember it said that the end of the world could happen at the turn of the millennium. We are still here. There is really no use trying to predict the end of this world, because Jesus told us that no one knows when the end will happen.

I think that it is more important to be ready for our end of the world, which will happen when we die. No one wants to die, but I do not think that death should be something to be feared. The end will come to all of us one day and I think it is important to be ready. Here are two things you need to do to prepare for death:

Love God with your whole being

Love your fellow human no matter if they be friend or enemy, as you love yourself.

Aside from that, everything else you do to prepare is unimportant. We should not sit waiting and worrying about the end times. We should live our lives with love, acceptance, forgiveness, compassion, and patience. If we live that way, we have nothing to worry about. In addition, we get a chance to live this way every day when we wake up to a new morning. God does not keep a scale, weighing sins against virtuous acts. Personally, I am very grateful for that.

Week 13-Sunday

Love for Enemies?

27"But I tell you who hear me: Love your enemies, do good to those who hate you, 28bless those who curse you, pray for those who mistreat you. 29If someone strikes you on one cheek, turn to him the other also. If someone takes your cloak, do not stop him from taking your tunic. 30Give to everyone who asks you, and if anyone takes what belongs to you, do not demand it back. 31Do to others as you would have them do to you.

32"If you love those who love you, what credit is that to you? Even 'sinners' love those who love them. 33And if you do good to those who are good to you, what credit is that to you? Even 'sinners' do that. 34And if you lend to those from whom you expect repayment, what credit is that to you? Even 'sinners' lend to 'sinners,' expecting to be repaid in full. 35But love your enemies, do good to them, and lend to them without expecting to get anything back. Then your reward will be great, and you will be sons of the Most High, because he is kind to the ungrateful and wicked. 36Be merciful, just as your Father is merciful" (Luke 6:27-36)

I was having a heated discussion at my hope and the subject came up about "Thou shall not kill." What does that mean? I take it to mean all killing, but my companions looked at it differently. Killing is OK if you are defending yourself; killing is OK if you are fighting in a "just war";

killing is OK to protect your family; killing is OK to defend our country; killing is OK if it is to protect your possessions.

So, if that is all true, why arn't those codicils in parentheses after the commandment. Is it possible that there is no time that is acceptable for killing? Is that what the law was written for? Jesus went further and discussed the killing of the spirit in a person being against God's will. Did he really mean all that, or is it OK to protect the "good" people by killing the bad? Moreover, who are the good among us and who are the bad? Sometimes the lines are very fuzzy between good and bad.

Let us think about this. How did Jesus demonstrate an answer to this question? Did he bring down destruction to those who were determined to kill him? Did he wipe them off the face of the earth, never to be seen again? I did not see that in the Gospel. Wouldn't that type of action make Jesus just like us? Moreover, what does it say about the "Kingdom of God"? Jesus let himself be killed for his belief and for his Father's Kingdom to be understood. They killed him, but he did not stay dead. He

rose and proved something to those who hated and killed him. He proved that God has power over death. He proved that the kingdom did not have to operate like our human kingdoms. When it looked as if he had failed in his mission, he rose from the dead bringing hope to all those who followed him then and now. We do not have to kill to win. The enemies of God will eventually lose because they cannot withstand the power of God.

Not only did Jesus preach goodness and love, he practiced it and demonstrated that God's Kingdom is the kingdom that will ultimately triumph over all kingdoms of earth. We should not be afraid to love our enemies; they really need God's love and help. If we stand with Jesus, and die with Jesus, we will also rise with Jesus. Think about it.

Week 14-Monday

We are united with God in Christ

6So then, just as you received Christ Jesus as Lord, continue to live in him, 7rooted, and built up in him, strengthened in the faith as you were taught, and overflowing with thankfulness.

8See to it that no one takes you captive through hollow and deceptive philosophy, which depends on human tradition and the basic principles of this world rather than on Christ.

9For in Christ all the fullness of the Deity lives in bodily form, 10and you have been given fullness in Christ, who is the head over every power and authority. 11In him you were also circumcised, in the putting off of the sinful nature,[a] not with a circumcision done by the hands of men but with the circumcision done by Christ, 12having been buried with him in baptism and raised with him through your faith in the power of God, who raised him from the dead". (Colossians 2:6-12)

Christianity is not a list of things to do. It is faith that Christ has done everything we need to be right with God; and he did it on the cross. "When we were God's enemies, we were reconciled to him through the death of his Son" (Romans 5:10). God reconciled the universe through Christ, "making peace through his blood, shed on the cross" (Colossians 1:20). If we are reconciled through him, all our sins are forgiven (verse 22)—reconciliation, forgiveness and justification all mean the same thing: peace with God.

The story does not end with the crucifixion. Friday was dark, but Sunday morning things brightened up considerably. If Jesus had just been killed, then it would have just been another example of a great human teacher being crushed by the status quo. He would have been no different than Socrates, Gandhi, or Martin Luther King. His death would have little meaning. However, Sunday Morning, the tomb was empty. In addition, for 40 days afterward Jesus was seen by more than 500 people (I Corinthians 15.6).

Just as the crucifixion is historical fact, so is the resurrection. Jesus lives today. In addition, he has a gift of eternal life available to everyone. Moreover, not just eternal life, but eternal relationship with God. Imagine, being on intimate terms with God, able to live in his presence and walk with him daily here on earth, but also to live forever with him in heaven. What would you pay for that opportunity? Well, it is not for sale. The price has already been paid.

Week 14-Tuesday

Will we recognize Jesus if he walked among us today?

5When Jesus looked up and saw a great crowd coming toward him, he said to Philip, "Where shall we buy bread for these people to eat?" 6He asked this only to test him, for he already had in mind what he was going to do.

7Philip answered him, "Eight months' wages[a] would not buy enough bread for each one to have a bite!"

8Another of his disciples, Andrew, Simon Peter's brother, spoke up, 9"Here is a boy with five small barley loaves and two small fish, but how far will they go among so many?"

10Jesus said, "Have the people sit down." There was plenty of grass in that place, and the men sat down, about five thousand of them. 11Jesus then took the loaves, gave thanks, and distributed to those who were seated as much as they wanted. He did the same with the fish.

12When they had all had enough to eat, he said to his disciples, "Gather the pieces that are left over. Let nothing be wasted." 13So they gathered them and filled twelve baskets with the pieces of the five barley loaves left over by those who had eaten. 14After the people saw the miraculous sign that Jesus did, they began to say, "Surely this is the Prophet who is to come into the world." 15Jesus, knowing that they intended to come and make him king by force, withdrew again to a mountain by himself." (John 6:5-15).

Would we recognize Jesus if he walked among us today? If someone performing signs and miracles were to suddenly, appear would we know for sure that it was Jesus?

If Jesus again walked among us, recognizing him would present a problem: The scriptures warn us that the working of signs and wonders mean absolutely nothing, because the Devil himself can duplicate these signs and wonders. The scriptures warn that even those who are called leaders in the Church will be deceived. Thus, the scriptures teach us that we are to ignore signs and wonders, and we cannot depend upon our religious leaders to recognize the return of the Christ.

This means the modern believer is confronted with a very serious problem that each of us must come to terms with. Once we acknowledge that we can neither rely upon either signs or our religious leaders, we are then left solely dependent upon our own wisdom and perception of the Word of God, which ultimately means, we must use the same exact test, as did the Jews to recognize the true Messiah when he comes. This presents a problem, in that, the only valid test which is ordained in the scriptures is to look for the one who will inaugurate the Kingdom of God.

In the realization of this fact, every Christian should ask himself what they would do today if we were confronted with the same exact problem as were the Jews at the beginning of our Common Era. What if a great teacher came and claimed to be the Messiah, performed miracles and signs, healed, and raised the dead, and yet he failed to fulfill the most important prophecy of scripture, and inaugurate the Kingdom of God upon the earth? Would we open our arms to him; hear his message; and alter our lives in accordance with his teachings? On the other hand, would we point to the warning of the scriptures, and like many of our Jewish brothers say: If you are indeed the Messiah, the Chosen One sent by God, then fulfill the scriptures, and inaugurate the Kingdom as the Bible foretells. However, what comprises the Kingdom of Heaven? How will we recognize that sign? What should we look for in the person who claims to be the returning Jesus? All of us would like to say that we would recognize Jesus. Probably most of the Jews thought the same thing. I think something to keep in mind is the distinct difference between Jesus and other religious leaders and miracle workers.

Jesus did not ask for anything for himself. Jesus did not ask for power, money, or fame. He did not destroy, he built. He did not condemn, he forgave. He did not judge, he loved. He only healed, he did not harm. I suppose if someone who possessed all those same characteristics would seem to fit the pattern of Jesus. However, I believe that we as his followers will know him in our hearts and souls.

We will recognize him by his love, his caring, his compassion, his acceptance of all who are forgotten.

Feeding the multitude was a sign of the power of Jesus while he walked the earth, but the bigger sign I think is the fact that he cared that the people were hungry and he cared about feeding them. He was concerned about the entire person and their needs. Jesus will feed both our bodies and our souls. We will know him by his love for us.

Week 14-Wednesday

Jesus Prays for All Believers

20"My prayer is not for them alone. I pray also for those who will believe in me through their message, 21that all of them may be one, Father, just as you are in me and I am in you. May they also be in us so that the world may believe that you have sent me? 22I have given them the glory that you gave me, that they may be one as we are one: 23I in them and you in me. May they be brought to complete unity to let the world know that you sent me and have loved them even as you have loved me. 24"Father, I want those you have given me to be with me where I am, and to see my glory, the glory you have given me because you loved me before the creation of the world. 25"Righteous Father, though the world does not know you, I know you, and they know that you have sent me. 26I have made you known to them, and will continue to make you known in order that the love you have for me may be in them and that I myself may be in them." (John 17:20-26)

Jesus prays for something of importance in this gospel. Jesus prays for us! "I do not pray for my disciples alone, I pray for all those who will believe in me through their word that they all may be one." Jesus prays for all those who believe in him. He prays for you and for me.

What does Jesus pray for? He prays, first, that we may be one. We are called to work for unity and harmony among all believers. Jesus also prays that we will be of one accord with God in all our thoughts and actions. He prays that we will always be in his company and that the love of God will always live in us.

That Jesus prays for us highlights the fact that we need prayers. Due to our fallen, wounded, nature, we cannot go it alone. Thankfully, the prayer of Jesus is effective. How could a loving Father not listen to the prayer of his only son? It is a great comfort to realize that Jesus prays for us. In good times and in bad, in sickness and in health, in happiness and depression, in success and failure, in sorrow, in doubt, in temptation, in all our sundry and varied needs, it is the prayer of Jesus that sustains us.

The knowledge that Jesus prays for us gives us the courage and fortitude to be all that God calls us to be. In times of failure and sin, Jesus gives us the hope and vision of ultimate success.

Gracious God,
you hear the prayers of Jesus, your Son,
who prays for us always,
even when we are weak and fail.

Help us to support each other
with the same love you have for us.
Without you, we can do nothing.
Amen.

Week 14-Thursday

The meaning of acceptance

"Am I now trying to win the approval of men, or of God? Or am I trying to please men? If I were still trying to please men, I would not be a servant of Christ" (Galatians 1:10).

The man or woman of God must learn that freedom from rejection and the praise of men comes from experiencing a greater acceptance and approval from Jesus. It allows you not only to accept others but also to have a greater confidence in Jesus. Jesus loves and accepts me even when I mess up, fail in my performance, and sin. Knowing that I am loved and accepted is my armor and shield of faith.

Perhaps you are facing a situation where you feel defeated by criticism, disapproval, humiliation, and exposure of your weaknesses. Tell Jesus how you feel. Clearly communicate your despair, discouragement, and frustration in prayer. Put your sense of hopelessness into words. Let Jesus know just how serious the situation has become for you. "Cast all your cares on him, for He cares for you" (1 Peter 5:7).

Then become part of a small group that can encourage and help you carry your burdens. Find some friends you can trust. Fear of rejection often makes accountability scary. However, no matter how deep the fear or how hard it may seem, a small group of friends will give you love, acceptance, and forgiveness rather than rejection. Their counsel will help you grow in Jesus and focus on the positive (Philippians 4:8). There are people who genuinely love you for who you are, not for something you can do for them. Cultivate these friends. Jesus will help you find them.

Christians who are trying to establish a healthy self-image for themselves are missing the point altogether. They are focusing on who they are in Christ, rather than on who Christ is in them. Instead, get caught up in reflecting the glory of Jesus instead of living the way of the Jesus. Behold the beauty of His majesty and glory. As you give yourself to beholding His face, you will not have any more problems with your self-image. You will forget about yourself and will be completely consumed with the beauty of His face.

Remember when we walk in his presence and behold his face and reflect his glory, we are changed into the likeness of Christ. Who else do we need to approve of us?

Week 14-Friday

Why did Jesus have to die?

30The God of our fathers raised Jesus from the dead—whom you had killed by hanging him on a tree. 31God exalted him to his own right hand as Prince and Savior that he might give repentance and forgiveness of sins to Israel. 32We are witnesses of these things, and so is the Holy Spirit, whom God has given to those who obey him." (Acts 5:30-32)

Jesus had an amazingly productive ministry, teaching and healing thousands. He attracted large crowds and had potential for much more. He could have healed thousands more by traveling to the Jews and gentiles who lived in other areas.

However, Jesus allowed this work to come to a sudden end. He could have avoided arrest, but he chose to die instead of expanding his ministry. Although his teachings were important, he had come not just to teach, but also to die, and he accomplished more in his death than in his life.

Death was Jesus' most important ministry. This is the way we remember him, through the cross as a symbol of Christianity or through the bread and wine of the Lord's Supper. Our Savior is a Savior who died.

For the transgression of my people, he was stricken...Though he had done no violence...it was the Lord's will to crush him and cause him to suffer...the Lord makes his life a guilt offering...He will bear their iniquities...He bore the sin of many, and made intercession for the transgressors (verses 4-12).

The Jewish leaders probably thought that Jesus' disciples would give up after their leader was killed. Moreover, it happened just as they hoped—the crucifixion shattered the disciples' hopes. They were dejected and said, "We had hoped that he was the one who was going to redeem Israel" (Luke 24:21). However, their hopes were dramatically restored when Jesus appeared to them after his resurrection, and at Pentecost, the Holy Spirit filled them with new conviction to proclaim salvation in Jesus Christ. They had unshakable faith in the least likely hero: a crucified Messiah.

Peter told the Jewish leaders; "The God of our fathers raised Jesus from the dead—whom you had killed by hanging him on a tree" (Acts 5:30). By using the word tree, Peter reminded the leaders of the curse of crucifixion. However, the shame was not on Jesus, he said—it was on the people who crucified him. God had blessed him because he did not deserve the curse he suffered. God had reversed the stigma.

Paul referred to the same curse in Galatians 3:13: "Christ redeemed us from the curse of the law by becoming a curse for us, for it is written: 'Cursed is everyone who is hung on a tree.'" Jesus became a curse on our behalf so we could escape the curse of the law. He became something he was not, so that we could become something we were not. "God made him who had no sin to be sin for us, so that in him we might become the righteousness of God" (2 Corinthians 5:21).

He became sin for us, so that we might be declared righteous through him. Because he suffered what we deserved, he redeemed us from the curse or penalty of the law. "The punishment that brought us peace was upon him." Because he suffered the penalty, we can enjoy peace with God.

Some have said that Jesus died to pay the legal demands of his Father—but it can also be said that the Father himself is the one who paid the price, by sending his Son for this very purpose (John 3:16; Romans 5:8). In Christ God absorbed the penalty himself, so that we did not have to. "By the grace of God he might taste death for everyone" (Hebrews 2:9).

Christianity is not a list of things to do. We do not belong to a club. Christianity is faith that Christ has done everything we need to be right with God, and he did it on the cross. "When we were God's enemies, we were reconciled to him through the death of his Son" (Romans 5:10). God reconciled the universe through Christ, "making peace through his blood, shed on the cross" (Colossians 1:20). If we are reconciled through him, all our sins are forgiven (verse 22)—

reconciliation, forgiveness and justification all mean the same thing: peace with God.

What looked like a shameful death for Jesus was actually a glorious triumph for God's plan; because it is through the cross, that Jesus won victory over enemy powers, including Satan, sin, and death. Their claim on us has been fully satisfied in the death of the innocent victim. They cannot demand any more than what he has already paid. They have nothing further to threaten us with.

"By his death," we are told, Jesus was able to "destroy him who holds the power of death—that is, the devil" (Hebrews 2:14). "The reason the Son of God appeared was to destroy the devil's work" (1 John 3:8). Victory was won on the cross.

Week 14-Saturday

Why did Jesus come to Earth?

John 3:17 "God did not send the Son into the world to judge the world, but that the world might be saved through Him."

John 6:38-40 "I have come down from heaven not to do my will but to do the will of him who sent me. And this is the will of him who sent me, that I shall lose none of all that he has given me, but raise them up at the last day. For my Father's will is that everyone who looks to the Son and believes in him shall have eternal life, and I will raise them up at the last day."

John 6:51 "I am the living bread that came down out of heaven; if anyone eats of this bread, he will live forever; and the bread that I will give for the life of the world is my flesh."

John 9:39 "For judgment I have come into this world, so that the blind will see and those who see will become blind."

John 10:10 "I came that they may have life, and have it abundantly."

John 12:46 "I have come as Light into the world, so that everyone who believes in Me will not remain in darkness."

John 18:37 Pilate said to Jesus, "You are a king?" Jesus answered, "You say correctly that I am a king. For this, I have been born, and for this, I have come into the world, to testify to the truth. Everyone who is of the truth hears My voice."

To many Christians, the word "ransom" sounds like sacrificial language, for we sometimes speak of Jesus as the ransom for our sins.

However, it almost certainly does not have this meaning in the two places that it is used in the Gospels. The Greek word translated as "ransom" (lutron) is used in the Bible not in the context of payment for sin, but to refer to payment made to liberate captives (often from captivity in war) or slaves (often from debt slavery). A lutron is a means of liberation from bondage.

Jesus came to liberate us from ourselves. Jesus came to demonstrate to us the way of living that would allow us to share the everlasting life of God.

Week 14-Sunday

Who is a disciple?

19Therefore go and make disciples of all nations, baptizing them in the name of the Father and of the Son and of the Holy Spirit, 20and teaching them to obey everything I have commanded you. (Matthew 28:19-20)

The English word, disciple, is derived from the Latin, discipulus, meaning “a learner or pupil; one who accepts and follows a given doctrine or teacher”. A disciple of Jesus Christ, therefore, is a person (male or female) who accepts and follows his teachings. All who are baptized in the name of the Triune God and accept that Jesus Christ is the Savior and Lord are Christians and, by definition, disciples.

Here is some further help answering the question “Who is a disciple?” A disciple is a person who has faith in Christ and their faith bears fruit through keeping the rules of “Love God and Love one another”: doing no harm by avoiding evil, doing good to all as often as possible, and practicing the means of gaining the grace of God through prayer, worship, taking part in the Lord’s Supper, reading and hearing Scripture, and performing acts of fasting and abstinence. Christian faith is exhibited by a life that strives toward holiness of heart and life (1 Thessalonians 3:11-13; Galatians 5:16-26; Ephesians 4:1-3; Philippians 2:12-13); perfection (maturity/ wholeness/ completeness) in love (Matthew 5:48; 1 John 2:3-6); “having the mind of Christ” (Philippians 2:5). A disciple is one whose life in the world is “faith working through love” (Galatians 5:6). A disciple’s life seeks wholehearted love for God through loving service in the world, especially with the poor, those who are sick, prisoners, lonely, tired, and lost (see Matthew 22:37-39; 25:31-46).

These are general rules for all Christians, regardless of denomination. They are simple, general, guides for living in the world as followers and friends of Jesus Christ. They are rules of life intended to help Christians to be mindful of the basics of loving God, loving neighbors and loving one another. They help disciples to attend to all of the teachings of Jesus and not only those that suit their temperament. A disciple, therefore, is a Christian who does his or her best to follow Jesus' teachings every day of the Week.

Week 15-Monday

Let there be Peace!

"Peace I leave with you; my peace I give you. I do not give to you as the world gives. Do not let your hearts be troubled and do not be afraid" (John 14:27).

The power "Peace on Earth" lies in our capacity to bring people of various cultures, faith traditions, and political ideals together as one united global heart and mind. The Message of Jesus allows us to sincerely focus on our mutual desire to serve, create, and manifest true peace on earth while transcending our differences and celebrating our common humanity.

This does not only include humankind but 'Life in all Realms of Creation'. When we speak the words, "Peace be with you," we should imagine that the frequency and energy field of Love, Peace and Harmony reaches throughout humanity and also throughout all of God's Creation.

Each of us must move to inspire, and re-awaken the inherit consciousness of love, peace and harmony which exists in everyone through Jesus. Jesus words of "Peace be with you," should direct our minds and hearts to bring inner peace of mind and consequently to foster peace in God's world at large.

Week 15-Tuesday

Jesus did not come to burden us.

28"Come to me, all you who are weary and burdened, and I will give you rest. 29Take my yoke upon you and learn from me, for I am gentle and humble in heart, and you will find rest for your souls. 30For my yoke is easy and my burden is light." (Matthew 11:28-30)

Sometimes it is very difficult to gain an understanding of all the rules and regulations of a particular Christian Church or religion. We might not be able to understand the reasoning as to why a church rule exists. We may feel that the rule is unfair. We may feel judged if we disagree with a position or direction of our particular church or congregation. We may even feel that we cannot live up to the demands placed upon us by our particular Christian denomination.

This is not the case with the message of Jesus. His message of love and Kingdom is very clear. There are no hidden meanings or unfairness of any kind. There are no complications or exceptions. His message is kind, loving, and gentle. One does not have to be a scholar to understand the meaning of His message. One could be a fisherman, or a tax collector, or even a tentmaker, and still be able to spread the Good News of Jesus. Furthermore following the instructions of Jesus will not be so demanding that one cannot possibly fulfill all of His expectations. We are allowed to fail and to try again. The simplicity of His loving message to us can be summed up in this message from the Gospel of Matthew.

Jesus did not come to burden us, but only to free us from the burdens we place upon ourselves.

Week 15-Wednesday

In the beginning…

26 Then God said, "Let us make man in our image, in our likeness, and let them rule over the fish of the sea and the birds of the air, over the livestock, over all the earth, [a] and over all the creatures that move along the ground."

27 So God created man in his own image,
In the image of God, he created him;
Male and female he created them.

28 God blessed them and said to them, "Be fruitful and increase in number; fill the earth and subdue it. Rule over the fish of the sea and the birds of the air and over every living creature that moves on the ground."

29 Then God said, "I give you every seed-bearing plant on the face of the whole earth and every tree that has fruit with seed in it. They will be yours for food. 30 And to all the beasts of the earth and all the birds of the air and all the creatures that move on the ground—everything that has the breath of life in it—I give every green plant for food." And it was so.

31 God saw all that he had made, and it was very good. And there was evening, and there was morning—the sixth day.

God did not look back on his creation and say: 1. I could have done better; or 2. It looked OK; 3. what was I thinking when I created those people, they are going to be trouble. No, the story goes that God was very pleased with his creation. Therefore, why can't we seem to see each other as being "very good"? We are all made in God's image. I do not believe that means our outer appearance is like God's outer appearance. We are made in God's image because our soul or spirit is part of God's Spirit. We are all given spirit from the same source.

In addition, God gave us the gift of free will. Our free will is like God's free will. We have the freedom to say yes and the freedom to say no. We just have not learned to say yes to the right things; that is our human condition. However, we should not lose hope. Since we have God's Spirit within us, we have the help that we need to say "yes" to the right things. God is always there to help us if we ask and allow him to do so.

Just as a parent is looking to support their child's first step, God is there to help our steps along life's way. Just as the child tries to walk on her own, we try to get through life on our own. However, God waits patiently for us to reach out to him.

We must not think that we have the exclusive rights to God's love and assistance. God has many, many children. Even though we fight each other, we have to realize that the people who fight us are God's children too. The people we do not like are God's children too. There is not one human that you see during your day who is not a child of God.

We should rejoice for the gift of one another and the differences in each other. God does!

Week 15-Thursday

Trust in God

Psalm 37 of David.
1 Do not fret because of evil men
or be envious of those who do wrong;
2 for like the grass they will soon wither,
like green plants they will soon die away.
3 Trust in the LORD and do good;
dwell in the land and enjoy safe pasture.
4 Delight yourself in the LORD
and he will give you the desires of your heart.
5 Commit your way to the LORD;
trust in him and he will do this:
6 He will make your righteousness shine like the dawn,
the justice of your cause like the noonday sun.
7 Be still before the LORD and wait patiently for him;
do not fret when men succeed in their ways,
when they carry out their wicked schemes.
8 Refrain from anger and turn from wrath;
do not fret—it leads only to evil.
9 For evil men will be cut off,
but those who hope in the LORD will inherit the land.
10 A little while, and the wicked will be no more;
though you look for them, they will not be found.
11 But the meek will inherit the land
and enjoy great peace.
12 The wicked plot against the righteous
and gnash their teeth at them;
13 but the Lord laughs at the wicked,
for he knows their day is coming.
14 The wicked draw the sword
and bend the bow

to bring down the poor and needy,
to slay those whose ways are upright.
15 But their swords will pierce their own hearts,
and their bows will be broken.

David had a great deal of confidence in God to protect and care for his people. He knew that there would be no future without God. He knew that even though it looks like evil may win the battle, they lose the war because of the strength of God. All evil would eventually perish, but those who stay faithful to God will live.

It is no different for us today. We see many tragic things happen in our world. We see war and death. We see famine and poverty. We see our fellow humans living under the peril of a government who does not believe in the sanctity of all human life. We see troubling times. We also think that this trouble is only happening to our current civilization. However, if you read Psalm 37, you see that God's people were experiencing similar situations in David's time.

Evil, pain, and suffering will always be with us. However, if we stay faithful to God, we will prevail over any tragedy that we experience. God is there with us and God is stronger than anything that is evil.

Trust in God, just as David did, and you will not be disappointed.

Week 15-Friday

Come Holy Spirit

Jesus Promises the Holy Spirit will be with us.

15"If you love me, you will obey what I command. 16And I will ask the Father, and he will give you another Counselor to be with you forever—+17the Spirit of truth. The world cannot accept him, because it neither sees him nor knows him. But you know him, for he lives with you and will be in you. 18I will not leave you as orphans; I will come to you. 19Before long, the world will not see me anymore, but you will see me. Because I live, you also will live. 20On that day you will realize that I am in my Father, and you are in me, and I am in you. 21Whoever has my commands and obeys them, he is the one who loves me. He who loves me will be loved by my Father, and I too will love him and show myself to him." (John 14:15-21)

The Holy Spirit is one of the three persons of God: Father, Son, and Holy Spirit. For many of us, this is a difficult concept to grasp. The Bible declares that there is only one living God, yet we learn from scripture that He comprises three separate personages. One way to visualize this concept is to examine the nature of water (H2O). Water is a single compound that can exist in three states—liquid, ice, and vapor. An egg is another picture. It is comprised of the white, the yoke, and the shell, yet it is still one egg. Of course, by no means do these examples paint a complete picture of our God, but they are illustrative of the fact that His three "persons" in no way invalidate His oneness.

The Holy Spirit is not a vague, ethereal life force. He is not impersonal or unthinking. The Holy Spirit is a "person" equal in every way with God, the Father, and God, the Son. The Bible tells us that all the characteristics of God apparent in the Father and the Son are equally apparent in the Holy Spirit.

In John, we learn that the Holy Spirit is our Counselor and teacher: "But the Counselor, which is the Holy Spirit, whom the Father will send in my name, He will teach you all things, and bring all things to your remembrance, whatsoever I have said to you."

The Holy Spirit is the guiding light of our lives and the life of the Christian Church. When in doubt, pray to the Holy Spirit, that the Spirit will "teach you all things."

Week 15-Saturday

A Day without God is a Day without Light

"When Jesus spoke again to the people, he said, "I am the light of the world. Whoever follows me will never walk in darkness, but will have the light of life." (John 8:12)

Essentially Jesus' life was about bringing life to people. John 1:4 describes Jesus this way, "In him was life, and that life was the light of men." He brought life. This means he brought hope and restoration to a world of hopelessness and brokenness. He freed some from the prison of sickness, others from the loneliness of being an outcast or low class, and a few from the grips of death itself.

By his teachings, Jesus also freed people from ignorance concerning God, his kingdom, the meaning of obedience and the way of salvation. He also freed some from their sins by granting forgiveness. Most importantly, the life Jesus brings is rooted in his sacrificial act of offering himself on the cross to take away the guilt of sin. John declared, "Look, the Lamb of God, who takes away the sin of the world" (Jn. 1:29). Moreover, Jesus says of himself, "For the Son of Man did not come to be served, but to serve, and to give his life as a ransom for many" (Mk 10:45).

Jesus came to display all the goodness of God through his caring acts toward people. He came teaching truth. He came to light our way to the Kingdom of God. Jesus is the light of the world.

Week 15-Sunday

A Word to the Wise

Proverbs 12
1 Whoever loves discipline loves knowledge,
but he who hates correction is stupid.
2 A good man obtains favor from the LORD,
but the LORD condemns a crafty man.
3 A man cannot be established through wickedness,
but the righteous cannot be uprooted.
4 A wife of noble character is her husband's crown,
but a disgraceful wife is like decay in his bones.
5 The plans of the righteous are just,
but the advice of the wicked is deceitful.
6 The words of the wicked lie in wait for blood,
but the speech of the upright rescues them.
7 Wicked men are overthrown and are no more,
but the house of the righteous stands firm.
8 A man is praised according to his wisdom,
but men with warped minds are despised.
9 Better to be a nobody and yet have a servant
than pretend to be somebody and have no food.
10 A righteous man cares for the needs of his animal,
but the kindest acts of the wicked are cruel.
11 He who works his land will have abundant food,
but he who chases fantasies lacks judgment.
12 The wicked desire the plunder of evil men,
but the root of the righteous flourishes.
13 An evil man is trapped by his sinful talk,
but a righteous man escapes trouble.
14 From the fruit of his lips a man is filled with good things
as surely as the work of his hands rewards him.
15 The way of a fool seems right to him,

but a wise man listens to advice.
16 A fool shows his annoyance at once,
but a prudent man overlooks an insult.
17 A truthful witness gives honest testimony,
but a false witness tells lies.
18 Reckless words pierce like a sword,
but the tongue of the wise brings healing.
19 Truthful lips endure forever,
but a lying tongue lasts only a moment.
20 There is deceit in the hearts of those who plot evil, but joy for those who promote peace.
21 No harm befalls the righteous,
but the wicked have their fill of trouble.
22 The LORD detests lying lips,
but he delights in men who are truthful.
23 A prudent man keeps his knowledge to himself,
but the heart of fools blurts out folly.
24 Diligent hands will rule,
but laziness ends in slave labor.
25 An anxious heart weighs a man down,
but a kind word cheers him up.
26 A righteous man is cautious in friendship,
but the way of the wicked leads them astray.
27 The lazy man does not roast his game,
but the diligent man prizes his possessions.
28 In the way of righteousness there is life;
along that path is immortality.

As I read these wise sayings, it occurred to me that even though these were written centuries ago, they are still true. I am especially fond of number 18.

" Reckless words pierce like a sword,
but the tongue of the wise brings healing."

I think it says that you should think before you speak. Words that you say to someone can live with him or her for the rest of their lives. I am sure that everyone has running around in their heads, words spoken to them that will never go away, good, or bad.

Jesus always used words very carefully. He thought before he spoke. He touched people with his words; he always spoke with love.

We have the power to touch someone's heart with love, or with hate. We can build up a person by saying the right thing, or we can destroy them forever. Words are important. The closer in relationship you are to someone, the more hurt, or healing can come from your words to them or from their words to you. Criticism must be tempered with love and compassion.

We must think like Jesus. Before we criticize, we should stop and think. I believe that we should look to be a positive memory in someone's life; a memory of love and compassion.

Week 16-Monday

Do not be Afraid

Psalm 20
A psalm of David.
1 May the LORD answer you when you are in distress;
may the name of the God of Jacob protect you.
2 May he send you help from the sanctuary
and grant you support from Zion.
3 May he remember all your sacrifices
and accept your burnt offerings.
Selah
4 May he give you the desire of your heart
and make all your plans succeed.
5 We will shout for joy when you are victorious
and will lift up our banners in the name of our God.
May the LORD grant all your requests.
6 Now I know that the LORD saves his anointed;
he answers him from his holy heaven
with the saving power of his right hand.
7 Some trust in chariots and some in horses,
but we trust in the name of the LORD our God.
8 They are brought to their knees and fall,
but we rise up and stand firm.
9 O LORD, save the king!
Answer us when we call!

This psalm is a prayer written by David, probably for use by all of Israel to pray for David himself and his army when they went into battle. This may seem presumptuous: David writes a prayer for others to pray, concerning himself. But rather than presumptuous, I think it shows the value that David placed on prayer. David knew that prayer was his best weapon when he went into battle. And so, David gave the people of Israel who stayed behind a prayer to pray. Through the important work of prayer, even those staying behind could share in the victory.

This can be a model prayer for us to pray for our political leaders as they lead our nation in battles of various kinds, as well as our spiritual leaders as they lead us in the spiritual warfare in which we are engaged. Our leaders need our prayers. Even the greatest leaders (especially the greatest leaders!) are subject to physical and spiritual trouble.

Paul tells us: "Everyone must submit himself to the governing authorities, for there is no authority except that which God has established. The authorities that exist have been established by God" (Rom. 13:1). Moreover, God wants us to pray for our leaders, even those we do not agree with: "I urge, then, first of all, that requests, prayers, intercession and thanksgiving be made for everyone—for kings and all those in authority, that we may live peaceful and quiet lives in all godliness and holiness. This is good, and pleases God our Savior, who wants all men to be saved and to come to a knowledge of the truth" (I Tim. 2:1-4).

This prayer of David's is also an excellent prayer for any of us to use for all our brothers or sisters who are facing battles, trials, or affliction. I know that in my own life I am asked by family, friends, and neighbors to pray for them, especially in their times of trouble. We must never forget that God is walking with us on this journey of life. Ask for God's help for others and for yourself as you are faced with the difficulties of life. God hears and answers all prayers.

Week 16-Tuesday

Does the world know that you are a follower of Jesus?

34"Then the King will say to those on his right, 'Come, you who are blessed by my Father; take your inheritance, the kingdom prepared for you since the creation of the world. 35For I was hungry and you gave me something to eat, I was thirsty and you gave me something to drink, I was a stranger and you invited me in, 36I needed clothes and you clothed me, I was sick and you looked after me, I was in prison and you came to visit me.'

37"Then the righteous will answer him, 'Lord, when did we see you hungry and feed you, or thirsty and give you something to drink? 38When did we see you a stranger and invite you in, or needing clothes and clothe you? 39When did we see you sick or in prison and go to visit you?'

40"The King will reply, 'I tell you the truth, whatever you did for one of the least of these brothers of mine, you did for me." (Matthew 25:34-39)

Spirituality involves living out the details in daily life of the religious beliefs one holds. One of the criticisms that is brought against those who profess to be Christian is that it can be too inward looking, forgetful of the needs of the world in which we live. A truly spiritual person is one who is transformed inwardly and so moves outwardly in compassion to the greater needs of others. All the great religions of the world have love of God and love of neighbor as the litmus test of the holy person.

So how do we live out our lives as true followers of Jesus?

Prayer is necessary to maintain our relationship with Jesus. However, we cannot forget the rest of the mission. Jesus prayed to his father and that is written very often in the Scriptures. However, Jesus was also compassionate, caring, forgiving, and most of all loving. His loving and healing ministry was very visible. Therefore, as true followers, we must make our lives in this world a visible expression of our Christianity.

Week 16-Wednesday

Who would you die for?

"You see, at just the right time, when we were still powerless, Christ died for the ungodly. Very rarely will anyone die for a righteous man, though for a good man someone might possibly dare to die. But God demonstrates his own love for us in this: While we were still sinners, Christ died for us". (Romans 5:6-8)

Jesus' death on the cross was the ultimate testimony of love. It is very easy to say, "I love you," but what does that really mean when we tell someone that. Love should not be selfish as in "I love you because you can do something for me," or even "I love you because you love me." Jesus' testimony to love what that he loved those who betrayed him. He loved without expecting love in return. He loved and was able to give up the most important aspect of his being, his own life. You cannot give up more than that to someone you love.

When we say we love, what does that mean we are willing to give up? It is something to think about. Jesus showed us that true love has no bounds. True love does not ask for anything in return. Loving someone may mean that we have to empty ourselves for the sake of someone else.

As Paul says in Romans, that Jesus gave us his life without looking for a reward; he gave up his life to those who really did not deserve his love; he gave up his life without the expectation of being loved in return.

Jesus showed us what it really means to love.

What a gift we have been given. We have received and still receive the gift of life from Jesus. His death brought us life.

Who would you give up your life for? Family? Friends? Strangers? Again, it is something to think about.

Week 16-Thursday

The Unchanging Ethics and Morality of Jesus

"Therefore everyone who hears these words of mine and puts them into practice is like a wise man who built his house on the rock. The rain came down, the streams rose, and the winds blew and beat against that house; yet it did not fall, because it had its foundation on the rock. But everyone who hears these words of mine and does not put them into practice is like a foolish man who built his house on sand. The rain came down, the streams rose, and the winds blew and beat against that house, and it fell with a great crash" (Matthew 7:24-27).

These moral and ethical behaviors are so explicit that we must consider them unequivocal in nature. They were not just behaviors to be observed by the people of the 1st century. Jesus reminds every generation and century of how one must live in the Kingdom of God. In addition to loving God, we must love one another. This is the part of the commandment that we seem to have a great deal of trouble with: "love one another." Yet Jesus laid out a roadmap for us to follow, the highlights of which are:

Love your enemies and do good to those who persecute you
Pray for forgiveness and forgive others
No one can serve two masters.
Does not judge or you too will be judged?

Jesus is the gravitational pull that brings everything together and gives them significance, reality, and meaning. Without Him, all things lose their value. Without Him, all things are but detached pieces floating around in space. It is not possible to emphasize a spiritual truth, value, virtue, or gift, yet miss Jesus, who is the embodiment and incarnation of all spiritual truth, values, virtues, and gifts. Seek Jesus, embrace Jesus, know Jesus, and you have touched Him who is Life. Moreover, in him resides all Truth, Values, Virtues, and Gifts in living color. Beauty has its meaning in the beauty of Jesus, in whom is found all that makes us lovely and loveable.

It is crucial to remember that our security can only be found in trusting Jesus with all that we are and have, being certain that He will never fail us. However, the Scriptures assure us that the Lord never gives up even when we fail in our commitment to follow him. He continually reaches out to re-invite us to follow him, and to find real peace in the journey.

Week 16-Friday

How do we die to self?

"I beseech you therefore, brothers and sisters, by the mercies of God, that you present your bodies a living sacrifice, holy, acceptable to God, which is your reasonable service. And do not be conformed to this world, but be transformed by the renewing of your mind, that you may prove what is that good and acceptable and perfect will of God. (Romans 12:1-2)

So, how do we truly present ourselves to God as a living sacrifice? Briefly, we must die to our prior selves. This concept is wonderfully presented in this anonymous poem:

"When you are forgotten, neglected, or purposely set at naught, and you don't sting or hurt with the oversight, but your heart is happy being counted worthy to suffer for Christ; that is dying to self.

When your good is evil spoken of, when your wishes are crossed, your advice disregarded, your opinion ridiculed, and you refuse to let anger rise in your heart or even defend yourself, but take it all in patient, loving silence; that is dying to self.

When you lovingly and patiently bear any disorder, any irregularity, and any annoyance; when you can stand face to face with waste, folly, extravagance, spiritual insensibility, and endure it as Jesus did; that is dying to self.

When you are content with any food, any climate, any society, any solitude, any interruption by the will of God; that is dying to self.

When you never care to refer to yourself in conversation or record your own good works or itch after commendation, when you can truly love to be unknown; that is dying to self.

When you can see your brother prosper and have his needs met, and can honestly rejoice with him in spirit and feel no envy, nor question God, while your own needs are far greater and you are in desperate circumstances; that is dying to self.

When you can receive correction and reproof from one of less stature than yourself and can humbly submit, inwardly as well as outwardly, finding no rebellion or resentment rising up within your heart; that is dying to self".

Week 16-Saturday

Rest in God's Love and Strength
1 God is our refuge and strength,
an ever-present help in trouble.
2 Therefore we will not fear, though the earth give way
and the mountains fall into the heart of the sea,
3 though its waters roar and foam
and the mountains quake with their surging.
Selah
4 There is a river whose streams make glad the city of God,
the holy place where the Most High dwells.
5 God is within her, she will not fall;
God will help her at break of day.
6 Nations are in uproar, kingdoms fall;
he lifts his voice, the earth melts.
7 The LORD Almighty is with us;
the God of Jacob is our fortress.
Selah
8 Come and see the works of the LORD,
the desolations he has brought on the earth.
9 He makes wars cease to the ends of the earth;
he breaks the bow and shatters the spear,
he burns the shields with fire.
10 "Be still, and know that I am God;
I will be exalted among the nations,
I will be exalted in the earth."
11 The LORD Almighty is with us;
the God of Jacob is our fortress.
(Psalm 46)

This Psalm 46 is a tribute to God's love and the writer's trust that God will always be our strength. However, how do we gain this faith and comprehension of God's love and protection?

The answer to that question is prayer. Prayer is our way to communicate with God, but it should not be a one-way conversation where we talk and God listens. The conversation should go both ways. Conversation is a commitment to falling more and more in love with God. The practice of prayer challenges us to let go of our agendas and make room for God to surprise us with our truth and the truth of others. We commit not only to speak to God, but also to listen to him. Normal conversation goes both ways and in our desire to develop a relationship with God, we must both speak and listen.

The fundamental stance of the person of faith is to listen. When we practice listening, we become more and more aware of the internal and external things that distract us. We listen with the ear of our heart the word heart does not simply refer to a physical organ or the seat of our emotions. It also includes other layers of meaning, such as inner understanding, feelings, will, desire, conscience, and the seat of courage.

Contemplation in prayer joins us to the One who dwells within, and enables us to see the world with God's eyes. The soul that is united with God can see the world with God's eyes. A true contemplative spirituality seeks to enter more fully into the depths of reality by resting in God's presence while God works in the soul.

We need to learn to rest in God's love and strength. Prayer and contemplation helps us to do just that.

Week 16-Sunday

Ten Things Christians Can Do.

Each of us is called to share our faith. We can no longer leave this work to the ordained, vowed, religious, and church professionals. Our mission in the workplace, the home, in social settings, and in the political arena is to proclaim and share the Good News. Take some time to reflect and discover your own response to the call to evangelize.

Ten things Christians can do for each other every day:

1. Treat others, as you would have them treat you:

Treat other people in the manner that you want them to treat you. This is a hallmark of Christianity. Be kind to people, even when they are unkind to you. That way, you set an example for them; you become a representative of the Christian faith.

"So in everything, do to others what you would have them do to you"—Jesus, as quoted in Matthew 7:12

2. Help people:

In Matthew 25:34-40, Jesus tells us that we are to give food to those who are hungry, give clothes to people who need them, provide shelter for people who have none, visit people who are sick, and give comfort to people who are in prison.

3. Don't worry:

Do your best. Deal with life's problems. However, do not worry. Instead, have faith in Jesus that all things will work out in the way they need to work out.

"Who of you by worrying can add a single hour to his life?"—Jesus, as quoted in Matthew 6:27

4. Read the Bible:

If you read the Bible contemplatively every day, especially the four Gospels, this practice will give you better insight into them life and teachings of Jesus, the Son of God.

5. Give thanks and be joyful:

"Be joyful always; pray continually; give thanks in all circumstances, for this is God's will for you in Christ Jesus." (1 Thessalonians 5:16-18)

6. Pray:

"*This, then, is how you should pray:*
'Our Father in heaven,
hallowed be your name,
your kingdom come,
your will be done
on earth as it is in heaven.
Give us today our daily bread.
Forgive us our debts,
as we also have forgiven our debtors.
And lead us not into temptation,
but deliver us from evil.' "

—Jesus, explaining how people should pray, as quoted in Matthew 6:9-13

7. Forgive your enemies:

"For if you forgive men when they sin against you, your heavenly Father will also forgive you. But if you do not forgive men their sins, your Father will not forgive your sins."

—Jesus, as quoted in Matthew 6:14-15

8. Be careful what you say about other people:

"But I tell you that men will have to give account on the day of judgment for every careless word they have spoken. For by your words you will be acquitted, and by your words you will be condemned."

—Jesus, as quoted in Matthew 12:36-37

9. Know the Word of God and use it each day:

If you read the four Gospels—Matthew, Mark, Luke, and John, you will see many examples of how Christians should act.

"Therefore everyone who hears these words of mine and puts them into practice is like a wise man who built his house on the rock."—Jesus, as quoted in Matthew 7:24

10. Be Christ for one another:

If you have found peace and salvation in the Bible, share it with others—tell people, write a letter, or create a Web site. Encourage others to read the Bible. Encourage family members and friends to attend church with you. Consider giving Bibles as gifts to others.

In addition, always, pray for God's assistance in your evangelization efforts.

"Therefore go and make disciples of all nations, baptizing them in the name of the Father and of the Son and of the Holy Spirit, and teaching them to obey everything I have commanded you. And surely I am with you always, to the very end of the age."—Jesus, as quoted in Matthew 28:19-20

Week 17-Monday

The heavenly King reigns in His people on earth

"I have been crucified with Christ; it is no longer I who live, but Christ lives in me; and the life which I now live in the flesh I live by faith in the Son of God, who loved me and gave Himself for me." (Galatians 2:20)

"For indeed, the kingdom of God is 'within you." (Luke 17:20)

"...you will know that I am in My Father, and you in me, and I in you. He who has my commandments and keeps them, it is he who loves me. And he who loves me will be loved by My Father, and I will love him and manifest myself to him." (John 14:20-21)

"If anyone loves me, he will keep my word; and My Father will love him, and we will come to him and make our home with him. He who does not love me does not keep my words." John 14:23-24

"Abide in Me, and I in you. As the branch cannot bear fruit of itself, unless it abides in the vine, neither can you, unless you abide in me. I am the vine, you are the branches. He who abides in me, and I in him, bears much fruit; for without me you can do nothing. If anyone does not abide in me, he is cast out as a branch and is withered..." John 15:4-6

Could the reason many of us Christians live poorly is because our understanding of the Gospel has more to do with going to heaven someday than becoming part of Jesus movement now?

Does your understanding of the good news of the Kingdom of Heaven align with Jesus'?

If we understood the Gospel as the arrival of Jesus' kingdom, where we have connected with Jesus to learn His teachings, to love God by loving our neighbor, and proclaim the healing of the cross and resurrection starting now, for "the Kingdom of Heaven is at hand".

Would the people of Jesus look different, live different, and become a better witness for others?

Many people who have studied and applied his teachings throughout history have given Jesus the title of the Great Teacher. The surprising thing is that Jesus was not the typical philosopher or preacher that people were used to. Unlike some other people Jesus tried to make His advice understandable to the common man, sometimes using stories or symbols, but always keeping His message simple, straightforward and practical.

So why is it that the message of the kingdom escapes so many of us?

Make no mistake; the Kingdom of Heaven is here. We do not have to wait for death to enter the kingdom. If you follow the teachings of Jesus, you have entered the kingdom. We help to create the kingdom in our homes, our communities, and our work. So where is the kingdom? It is everywhere you look right here on earth.

Week 17-Tuesday

We Become Signs of God's Love

"Jesus answered him, "If I do not wash your feet, you have no share with me." (John 13:8)

To be spiritual means to live according to the knowledge that Jesus is present to us in the world helping us to work toward a personal, interpersonal, social, and even perhaps cosmic transformation. He is not just a historical figure; He lives in each one of us. We are relational beings and to be spiritually Christian we must live always in relations with God, our neighbor, our world and ourselves, following the example left to us by Jesus. We must be willing to love and serve those around us. We must allow his Spirit to work through us individually and collectively to transform the world so that we may bring forth the Kingdom of God here on earth.

For those of us who choose to follow Jesus, we make a choice to give up our life of selfishness and follow a life of love. The perfection of this love has to be the purpose of this life. The decision to become models of Jesus' message of unconditional love is one of the most important choices of our lives. It is a radical decision. After all, the consequence of Jesus' love for us brought Him to a death on the cross.

In our quest for true spirituality, Jesus speaks in to our darkness with His eternal message of love. We all long for true spiritual connections that transcend our hurried existence and from which we can leave our world of temporary and changing and secure a sense of permanent and unchangeable. We can only receive this security by developing our relationship with God/Jesus. Security will not come from a new age therapy, from the accumulation of wealth, nor from any of our earthly relationships. We must come to Jesus, embracing our spiritual bankruptcy and brokenness, and seeking His love and acceptance. We cannot come to Him on our terms, but come to Him on His terms.

"To see past apparent differences among people, we must look with spiritual eyes, not with earthbound eyes of flesh, because it is the spirit that gives life, the flesh is of no avail. In the same way we must look with eyes of the spirit at the bread of the Lord's table, trusting completely his words, words that are spirit and life." (John 6:63)

Week 17-Wednesday

You Must Experience a Rebirth in Christ

"That you may be children of your Father in heaven. He causes his sun to rise on the evil and the good, and sends rain on the righteous and the unrighteous" (Matthew 5:45).

The teaching, that you may be children of your Father in heaven requires us to act on our love of our enemies. The highest reward goes only to those who meet this high ethical and moral standard. When one holds the values expressed in the Beatitudes, one becomes like the Lord, mentally and spiritually. Symbolically, the New Testament speaks of this as a new birth. John records Jesus' explanation of this spiritual birth:

"Jesus answered, 'I tell you the truth, no one can enter the kingdom of God unless he is born of water and the Spirit. Flesh gives birth to flesh, but the Spirit gives birth to spirit. You should not be surprised at my saying, "You must be born again" (John 3:5-7).

Paul described how the birth occurs in his letter to the Romans:

"Or don't you know that all of us who were baptized into Christ Jesus were baptized into his death? We were therefore buried with him through baptism into death in order that we may rise with Him"(Romans 6:3-40).

Although this rising with Jesus is difficult, we need to remember that we do not have to do this alone. In order to experience a rebirth with Jesus, we must rely on Jesus to help us experience this rebirth. We need to realize that must place our trust and faith in Jesus in order to share in Jesus' life. Ask, and for help and it will be given to you.

Week 17-Thursday

What is the Good News Jesus came to tell us?

Jesus came to bring us the good news of salvation. However, what does salvation mean? Throughout the New Testament, the words "save," "saved," and "salvation" have their root in the Greek "sozo" which means to save, to rescue, to deliver, to protect. "Sozo" is also translated in the New Testament with the words heal, preserve, save, do well, and to make whole. The Greek "soteria" (which has its origin in "sozo") is the main word translated "salvation." "Soteria" is also translated to deliver, health, salvation, save and saving.

One can learn the full meaning of a Greek word by studying the scriptures where it is used and the way it is interpreted. You can easily see from the previous definitions that "salvation" means much more than a soul's preparation for Heaven.

In Romans 1:16-17, the Apostle Paul writes, "For I am not ashamed of the gospel of Christ; for it is the power of God for salvation ("soteria") to everyone that believes...For there is the righteousness of God revealed from faith to faith."

Jesus came to bring us salvation, which means He came to rescue, deliver, protect, heal, and save us. He came to make us whole and to reconnect us with the God who loves us. He came so save us from our sin, our despair, our loneliness, our fear and our lack of faith (Mark 4:35-41).

After living in Nazareth for thirty years (Luke 3:23), Jesus began to deliver His message, which was called the Good News (Matthew 4:23). What was the Good News? In the time of Jesus, the people were burdened with laws that regulated the smallest layers of daily life. Besides the oppressive laws of their Roman conquerors, there was the body of Jewish law. There were not just Ten Commandments; there were 613 commandments and 365 prohibitions. When they could not measure up to the laws, the religious leaders cut them off from the society of decent people.

Jesus told people He had come to fulfill that prophecy, to bring them the Good News for which they had waited for so long (Luke 4:20-21). Part of the Good News brought to us by Jesus was that being fully human in the true sense of the word was true holiness. Not all the commandments and prohibitions made one holy. Being what God created us to be, just ourselves, good human beings was what made one holy (Mark 4:35-41). There is a profound revelation in that, and an important part of the Good News, that you could be ordinary, doing the ordinary, everyday things that people do, and underneath that simple, ordinary persona, possess extraordinary holiness.

How Jesus lived His own life as a human shows how we are to live ours (John 16:25-28). In His own life, Jesus lived simply. He was deeply in love with everything and everyone living, from God down to the simplest creature. He was gentle and compassionate, especially to those who were ostracized by society (Mark 2:17). He never gave an appearance of self-righteousness, but had a genuine humility and meekness and an understanding of others.

Jesus loves all of us as we are and reaches us where we are. That is the beauty of the Good News. We are OK to be where we are. We can be ourselves. We do not have to become like anyone else to be loved by Jesus.

Week 17-Friday

We are not servants, but friends.

9"As the Father has loved me, so have I loved you. Now remain in my love. 10If you obey my commands; you will remain in my love, just as I have obeyed my Father's commands and remain in his love. 11I have told you this so that my joy may be in you and that your joy may be complete. 12My command is this: Love each other as I have loved you. 13Greater love has no one than this that he lay down his life for his friends. 14You are my friends if you do what I command. 15I no longer call you servants, because a servant does not know his master's business. Instead, I have called you friends, for everything that I learned from my Father, I have made known to you. 16You did not choose me, but I chose you and appointed you to go and bear fruit—fruit that will last. Then the Father will give you whatever you ask in my name. 17This is my command: Love each other" (John 15:9-17).

The freedom and peace Jesus talked about had to do not only with material things, but also with anything that generated undue anxiety. Despite the constant turmoil that surrounded Jesus, from the angry religious leaders to the constant crowds pressing in on Him, He displayed a remarkable calmness that proved the value of detachment that Jesus had from whatever could disturb His inner peace. The promise of peace was a promise Jesus wanted to share with His followers (John 14:27).

As concerned as Jesus was about spreading His Good News, He is not compulsive or driven like so many people with a mission. He lived His life, enjoying each day, making new friends, and maintaining warm relationships with His old friends. This, too, could be considered part of His Good News. He taught by His example how people could live with joy and serenity, and not allow themselves to be so driven that they lose their peace of mind and sense of balance. Through it all, they can enjoy an intimate relationship with God, which is built into the essence of being fully human.

Week 17-Saturday

The Good News is that we are loved by God

36Now one of the Pharisees invited Jesus to have dinner with him, so he went to the Pharisee's house and reclined at the table. 37When a woman who had lived a sinful life in that town learned that Jesus was eating at the Pharisee's house, she brought an alabaster jar of perfume, 38and as she stood behind him at his feet weeping, she began to wet his feet with her tears. Then she wiped them with her hair, kissed them and poured perfume on them.

39When the Pharisee who had invited him saw this, he said to himself, "If this man were a prophet, he would know who is touching him and what kind of woman she is—that she is a sinner."

40Jesus answered him, "Simon, I have something to tell you."

"Tell me, teacher," he said.

41"Two men owed money to a certain moneylender. One owed him five hundred denarii, and the other fifty. 42Neither of them had the money to pay him back, so he canceled the debts of both. Now which of them will love him more?"

43Simon replied, "I suppose the one who had the bigger debt canceled."

"You have judged correctly," Jesus said.

44Then he turned toward the woman and said to Simon, "Do you see this woman? I came into your house. You did not give me any water for my feet, but she wet my feet with her tears and wiped them with her hair. 45You did not give me a kiss, but this woman, from the time I entered, has not stopped kissing my feet. 46You did not put oil on my head, but she has poured perfume on my feet. 47Therefore, I tell you, her many sins have been forgiven—for she loved much. But he who has been forgiven little loves little."

48Then Jesus said to her, "Your sins are forgiven."

49The other guests began to say among themselves, "Who is this who even forgives sins?"

50Jesus said to the woman, "Your faith has saved you; go in peace."

Jesus spoke in very down to earth parables about life, His values, and His vision of what our life could be. He preached a message of hope and freedom and salvation. He gathered thousands of people into a new community, a community in which there would be no vestige of the complex structure of laws, prohibitions, and rituals that had so burdened their lives. Setting people free was part of His main goal. Bringing people back to His Father's family was part of His gift to us.

Jesus realized that the life He was sharing was fragile and easily shattered, so He gave His apostles the authority to reconcile those who had drifted or damaged their friendship with God. He also gave His disciples food, which would nourish the divine life within them. He promised His followers that when they accepted His friendship, He and His Father would come and live within them (John 12:44-50).

The gift of God's living within us is the basis for the natural growth of the divine life received in baptism, except in many cases the relationship is not nourished. The intimacy with God was the source of Jesus' own strength in His humanity. It flowed from the rich prayer life that He nourished constantly. This is the secret to intimacy with God. We must maintain constancy in prayer, because it develops within the soul a communion and a sharing of thoughts and feelings between the soul and God.

On earth, Jesus tried to help people understand that God knows our weakness and our efforts. He understands our struggling, our pain, and our determination to do better. As long as we are sensitive to the pain and loneliness of others, and reach out to heal, our own sins, as many as they may be, will be forgiven. This is the Good News!

Prayer
Loving Spirit of Wisdom,
guide our thoughts and our memories.

In the light of your love,
may we see what is important for us to remember,
what is important for us to hold to our hearts,
and what we need simply to let go of in peace.

For we trust you to be our guide
even when the path seems unclear to us.
Through Jesus Christ,
Amen.

Week 17-Sunday

When did you last see Jesus?

10Then the disciples went back to their homes, 11but Mary stood outside the tomb crying. As she wept, she bent over to look into the tomb 12and saw two angels in white, seated where Jesus' body had been, one at the head and the other at the foot.

13They asked her, "Woman, why are you crying?"

"They have taken my Lord away," she said, "and I don't know where they have put him." 14At this, she turned around and saw Jesus standing there, but she did not realize that it was Jesus.

15"Woman," he said, "why are you crying? Who is it you are looking for?"

Thinking he was the gardener, she said, "Sir, if you have carried him away, tell me where you have put him, and I will get him."

16Jesus said to her, "Mary."

She turned toward him and cried out in Aramaic, "Rabboni!" (Which means Teacher).

17Jesus said, "Do not hold on to me, for I have not yet returned to the Father. Go instead to my brothers and tell them, 'I am returning to my Father and your Father, to my God and your God.' "

18Mary Magdalene went to the disciples with the news: "I have seen the Lord!" And she told them that he had said these things to her…(John 20:10-18)

I want to share a line of thought with you that has often been with me and I hope it makes you as uncomfortable as it always makes me. I want to ask you a very searching question: When did you last see Jesus? Do I hear anybody say, 'What do you mean? Nobody has ever seen Jesus in our generation. They saw him 2000 years ago, but nobody sees him now?'

However, you see him every day…

Just as Mary did not recognize Jesus in the garden, we do not recognize Jesus when he appears in front of us as we go through our day. Jesus can appear as someone who need assistance, or as someone who in there to give assistance to us. We might see him at the grocery store, the bank, or the post office. Jesus is in all of those places. We need to recognize that Jesus is in each one of us.

That is the good news. You can have a personal encounter with the living Jesus. You come face to face with him when you experience love and mercy and when you experience forgiveness and pardon. That knowledge will revolutionize your life and you will never be the same again. There is no thrill like the thrill of knowing Jesus Christ. There is no emotional experience that can match the joy of knowing that you are loved.

Week 18-Monday

Is it better to be right, or is it better to be kind?

"Do not let any unwholesome talk come out of your mouths, but only what is helpful for building others up according to their needs, that it may benefit those who listen. And do not grieve the Holy Spirit of God, with whom you were sealed for the day of redemption. Get rid of all bitterness, rage and anger, brawling and slander, along with every form of malice. Be kind and compassionate to one another, forgiving each other, just as in Christ God forgave you" (Ephesians 4:29-32).

Kindness is a language the blind can see and the deaf can hear.
A kind and courteous "no" hurts less than a rude "yes."

Being correct does not give us the right feel superior. Nor does it mean that it is OK to degrade someone else. It is important to be forgiving, but it is also important to try not to do those things that cause us to seek forgiveness. Treating others, as we would like to be treated is not just a trite motto taught to schoolchildren, it should be a life rule for all those who follow Jesus. Sticks and stones can break bones, but name-calling can cause injury that lasts a lifetime.

I believe that it is important to remember how Jesus spoke to people. His words were filled with kindness and compassion. He was never cruel.

Therefore, as we go through our day, we should error on the side of love. Kindness and compassion goes a long way.

Week 18-Tuesday

Who do you turn to in times of trouble?

Matthew 19:26...[26] Jesus looked at them and said, "With man this is impossible, but with God all things are possible."

Faith is simply a response to the promises of God. His promises are not just words to hang on a wall; they require action on our part. Hebrews 13:5-6 provides a wonderful demonstration of how we should apply God's Word to our lives: here is the promise: "...for he has said, 'I will never leave you, nor forsake you.'" Here is how we should understand this: "...so that we may boldly say, 'The Lord is my helper, and I will not fear what man shall do to me.'" One of my favorites is 1 Chronicles 28:20—in this case, our response comes first: "And David said to Solomon his son, 'Be strong and of good courage, and do it: fear not, nor be dismayed.'" Here's the promise: "...'for the LORD God, even my God, will be with you; he will not fail you, nor forsake you, until you have finished all the work for the service of the house of the LORD.'"

As you face difficulties, dig into the Word of God and ask Him to direct you to specific passages that apply to your specific circumstances. After all, this is no dusty book we hold; it is alive. Through His Spirit, this living book is able to examine our heart as well as meet our needs—"...the Word of God is quick and powerful and sharper than any two-edged sword, piercing even to the dividing asunder of soul and spirit, and of the joints and marrow and is a discerner of the thoughts and intents of the heart" (Heb. 4:12).

So, in your troubles do your part. Ask the Lord for help and to reveal His will and plan for your life. Commit yourself fully to Him. Walk in obedience to His Word no matter what the cost. If you take this approach, God will provide for you in ways that go far beyond human understanding.

Have hope and be encouraged: God is with us. God is infinite. God is all-powerful, all knowing, and all capable. There are no limits restricting God. Yet despite this, to our own harm we, His followers tend to limit the power of God by erroneous thinking.

Week 18-Wednesday

The Gift that keeps on giving

17As Jesus started on his way, a man ran up to him and fell on his knees before him. "Good teacher," he asked, "what must I do to inherit eternal life?"

18"Why do you call me good?" Jesus answered. "No one is good—except God alone. 19You know the commandments: 'Do not murder, do not commit adultery, do not steal, do not give false testimony, do not defraud, honor your father and mother.' "

20"Teacher," he declared, "all these I have kept since I was a boy."

21Jesus looked at him and loved him. "One thing you lack," he said. "Go, sell everything you have and give to the poor, and you will have treasure in heaven. Then come, follow Me."

22At this the man's face fell. He went away sad, because he had great wealth.

23Jesus looked around and said to his disciples, "How hard it is for the rich to enter the kingdom of God!"

24The disciples were amazed at his words. But Jesus said again, "Children, how hard it is to enter the kingdom of God! 25It is easier for a camel to go through the eye of a needle than for a rich man to enter the kingdom of God."

26The disciples were even more amazed, and said to each other, "Who then can be saved?"

27Jesus looked at them and said, "With man this is impossible, but not with God; all things are possible with God." (Mark 10:17-27)

God has given each of us His perfect plan of salvation; Everlasting Life! It is His gift of grace to each one of us. We do not deserve it; we cannot buy it, and we cannot earn it…it is simply a gift! All we have to do is claim it.

"For God so loved the world, He gave His only begotten Son, that whoever believes in Him should not perish, but have everlasting life." (John 3:16)

God has given each of us a free will to decide how we will live our lives here on earth. We can opt for good or evil; we can follow a path of disobedience or a path of faithfulness…it is our decision. We have the power to accept or reject the gift.

We are not forgiven through trying our best to live a "good" life. We are forgiven by the great love of Jesus. God is willing to forgive us if we are willing to receive and accept His gift of grace and forgiveness in Jesus. .

Jesus Christ is our only path to eternal life with God, but you must open the door and invite Him into your life.

" *Behold, I stand at the door and knock. If anyone hears my voice and opens the door, I will come in to him and dine with him, and he with Me. (Rev. 3:20)*

If you believe in Jesus Christ and His gift to you of His life, please do not delay your decision any longer. Yield your life to Him right now. Invite Jesus to come through the doorway of your life. Your life will be miraculously changed, by simply, and earnestly praying to Jesus to be with you.

Realize that God loves you and believe that Jesus Christ died for you. Truly, the gift keeps on giving.

Week 18-Thursday

What is compassion?

.

1 Praise the LORD, O my soul;
all my inmost being, praise his holy name.
2 Praise the LORD, O my soul,
and forget not all his benefits-
3 who forgives all your sins
and heals all your diseases,
4 who redeems your life from the pit
and crowns you with love and compassion,
5 who satisfies your desires with good things
so that your youth is renewed like the eagle's.
6 The LORD works righteousness
and justice for all the oppressed.
7 He made known his ways to Moses,
his deeds to the people of Israel:
8 The LORD is compassionate and gracious,
slow to anger, abounding in love.
9 He will not always accuse,
nor will he harbor his anger forever;
10 he does not treat us as our sins deserve
or repay us according to our iniquities.
11 For as high as the heavens are above the earth,
so great is his love for those who fear him;
12 as far as the east is from the west,
so far has he removed our transgressions from us.
13 As a father has compassion on his children,
so the LORD has compassion on those who fear him;
14 for he knows how we are formed,
he remembers that we are dust.
15 As for man, his days are like grass,
he flourishes like a flower of the field;
16 the wind blows over it and it is gone,

and its place remembers it no more.
17 But from everlasting to everlasting
the LORD's love is with those who fear him,
and his righteousness with their children's children-
18 with those who keep his covenant
and remember to obey his precepts.

19 The LORD has established his throne in heaven,
and his kingdom rules over all.
20 Praise the LORD, you his angels,
you mighty ones who do his bidding,
who obey his word. 21 Praise the LORD, all his heavenly hosts,
you his servants who do his will.
22 Praise the LORD, all his works
everywhere in his dominion.
Praise the LORD, O my soul.
(Psalm 103 Of David)

David was expressing joy in feeling the compassion and goodness of God. He had felt God's love and compassion in his life and this psalm was definitely his expression of feeling that compassion from God. David recognized that God understood and cared about our pain and our struggles. Just as wisdom covers the intellectual or comprehending side of our nature, compassion covers the feeling side of our nature

Compassion is made up of two words. 'co' meaning together and 'passion' meaning a strong feeling. We are compassionate when we feel the pain of others. When we see someone is in distress and we feel their pain as if it were our own, and strive to eliminate or lessen their pain, then this is compassion. So all the best in human beings, all the Godlike qualities like sharing, readiness to give comfort, sympathy, concern and caring—all are manifestations of compassion.

You will notice also that in the compassionate person, care and love towards others has its origins in care and love for oneself. It is difficult to have compassion for others when we have none for ourselves. We can help others to see God's love in their lives only when we feel God's love for ourselves. We can feel the pain of others when we understand our own pain.

So in trying to walk in Jesus' footsteps, one's own spiritual development blossoms quite naturally from caring for ourselves into concern for the welfare of others. Once we have felt God's love and compassion for ourselves, it is then that we can share that love and compassion with others. You cannot give what you do not feel. You cannot fill others unless you are filled.

Jesus life and ministry illustrates this compassionate spirituality. Jesus could teach about God's love, because he felt it very strongly in his earthly life. He knew first-hand about God's love and compassion. His ministry was about sharing this great compassion with those who did not know the feeling of compassion. They had not experienced compassion in their own lives, so they did not know how to share it with others.

Always remember that God loves you. Rest your souls in God's loving compassion.

Week 18-Friday

God is always with us

15"If you love me, you will obey what I command. 16And I will ask the Father, and he will give you another Counselor to be with you forever—17the Spirit of truth. The world cannot accept him, because it neither sees him nor knows him. But you know him, for he lives with you and will be in you. 18I will not leave you as orphans; I will come to you. 19Before long, the world will not see me anymore, but you will see me. Because I live, you also will live. 20On that day you will realize that I am in my Father, and you are in me, and I am in you. 21Whoever has my commands and obeys them, he is the one who loves me. He who loves me will be loved by my Father, and I too will love him and show myself to him." (John 14:15-21)

God's love is always with us. In our darkest moments when we are doubled over in pain or grief, God's love is over us, under us, within us, and all around us. Even when we do not sense His love, His love is still with us. Because God is so much with us regardless of our circumstances, we can find His comfort at any time in any place. When you need God's love the most, He is with you. When you think you can handle all things on your own, He is with you knowing there will come a time when your ego is deflated and you will need Him more than ever. We can let our sin come between God and us. However, God does not forsake us.

God is always telling us to always turn to Him, always trust in Him, always believe in Him, and always have faith in Him…all because He always loves us. Although we cannot always express our love for Him, His love remains. Although we selfishly set conditions upon God's love for us, God always loves us unconditionally. Although we have spots and blemishes in our sin, God loves us in spite of our spots and blemishes. Although we do not always give God the praise and honor He deserves, He loves us in spite of our selfishness.

Although we think we have power, God still loves us even when He knows we are small and weak. Although we have burdens and needs interfering with God's love in us, His love always remains with us. Although our words are feeble when we talk with Him in prayer, He is always able to read our hearts in spite of our feeble words…because He always loves us and His love is always with us.

Week 18-Saturday

Love as Jesus loves

23"Jesus replied, "If anyone loves me, he will obey my teaching. My Father will love him, and we will come to him and make our home with him. 24He who does not love me will not obey my teaching. These words you hear are not my own; they belong to the Father who sent me". (John 14:23-24)

However, how do we show our love for one another? Well, how do you show someone close to you that you love them? There are many different responses to that, but eventually it all comes down to this: spending time with them. However, wait! Jesus also said in John 14 that "if you love me, you will obey my teaching." That certainly is true. We might take note of the order of his statement, however: if this, then that. Love comes before, and thus prompts, obedience. How will we know what to obey if we do not check in with him for orders first?

This is why an understanding of the Scriptures and prayer as central for the disciple of Jesus in having daily communion with God. There are many spiritual disciplines, but these two are foundational both in the life of Jesus and in Scripture itself.

We must develop the habit of spending time with God each day in two ways. Reading from his Word for wisdom, nurture, sharpening, help, etc. fills us with his instruction, shapes us for purity and action, and equips us to remain in his will and avoid the pitfalls of sin, which harm us. Spending time in prayer positions us for God to transform us by the Holy Spirit who does his work in us. It is time spent in both speaking and listening to God.

We also need to develop the human element of community made effective by Christ's presence among us. People need people; nobody needs to go it alone. Jesus taught that we need one another for help and support.

We are on the journey together, discovering real life from Jesus in community with one another.

Week 18-Sunday

God gives us all life and breath

24"The God who made the world and everything in it is the Lord of heaven and earth and does not live in temples built by hands. 25And he is not served by human hands, as if he needed anything, because he himself gives all men life and breath and everything else. 26From one man he made every nation of men, that they should inhabit the whole earth; and he determined the times set for them and the exact places where they should live. 27God did this so that men would seek him and perhaps reach out for him and find him, though he is not far from each one of us. 28'For in him we live and move and have our being.' As some of your own poets have said, 'We are his offspring.' (Acts 17:24-28)

Christianity is not just a religion. True Christians experience a deep personal relationship with the Creator God of the universe. The God of the Scriptures reaches out to people in love. He has provided a way for you to be united with Him. The way is through His Son, Jesus Christ.

A SALVATION PRAYER

Pray this prayer from your heart, and speak it aloud if you are able.

Lord Jesus, I believe that you are the Son of God and you became a man to suffer and die on a cross to pay the penalty for my sins, and I believe that you rose from the dead and you are alive, and you are Lord of the universe. I confess that I have sinned against you and against people, and I pray that you will forgive me and wash me clean through the blood that you shed on the cross. I pray that you and God the Father, and the Holy Spirit, will come and live in me and I will live in you. I give my life to you to do your will and not my will. Please give me the faith to believe all the promises that you have written to me in Your Word the Holy Bible. Lord Jesus please baptize me in the Holy Spirit and fill me with your presence. Please give me the strength and the faith to accomplish the plans and the destiny that you have for me and give me the courage to be a witness for you. Please fill me with your love and compassion for people so I can be likes You, I pray all these things in Jesus name, Amen.

Week 19-Monday

Be Compassionate as God is Compassionate

43"You have heard that it was said, 'Love your neighbor and hate your enemy.' 44But I tell you: Love your enemies and pray for those who persecute you, 45that you may be sons of your Father in heaven. He causes his sun to rise on the evil and the good, and sends rain on the righteous and the unrighteous. 46If you love those who love you, what reward will you get? Are not even the tax collectors doing that? 47And if you greet only your brothers, what are you doing more than others? Do not even pagans do that? 48Be perfect, therefore, as your heavenly Father is perfect." (Matthew 5:43-48)

I do not think that Jesus meant that we have to be perfect. Some translations of this passage substitute the word compassionate for the word perfect. We will never be perfect as God is perfect in all things. However, we can show compassion to others as God shows compassion to us.

Compassion is an emotion that is a sense of shared suffering, most often combined with a desire to alleviate or reduce the suffering of another; to show special kindness to those who suffer. Compassion essentially arises through empathy, and is often characterized through actions, wherein a person acting with compassion will seek to aid those they feel compassionate for.

The practice of compassion as Jesus talks about it, is not only wanting to ease the suffering of those we love, but even those who mistreat us. That is a tall order, so how do we do that? Here is a suggestion. When we encounter someone who mistreats us, instead of acting in anger, withdraw. Later, when you are calm and more detached, reflect on that person who mistreated you. Try to imagine the background of that person. Try to imagine what that person was taught as a child. Try to imagine the day or Week, that person was going through, and what kind of bad things had happened to that person. Try to imagine the mood and state of mind that person was in—the suffering that person must have been going through to mistreat you that way.

Moreover, understand that their action was not about you, but about what they were going through. Now think some more about the suffering of that poor person, and see if you can imagine trying to stop the suffering of that person. Then reflect that if you mistreated someone, and they acted with kindness and compassion toward you, whether that would make you less likely to mistreat that person the next time, and more likely to be kind to that person.

Once you have mastered this practice of reflection, try acting with compassion and understanding the next time a person mistreats you. Do it in little doses, until you are good at it. Practice makes perfect.

Week 19-Tuesday

Kingdom living? Now or Later?

"For, behold, the kingdom of God is within you," (Luke 17:21).

How does His kingdom become a part of you? Within you? The kingdom of God is a Spiritual realm, attained by walking in God's Spirit, and producing the fruit of the Spirit, which is love, joy, peace, longsuffering, kindness, goodness, faithfulness, gentleness, and self-control. We obtain these characteristics from walking in His Spirit. This holds true today as it did in the 1st century.

There are the Beatitudes that are results of kingdom living and walking in His Spirit, not suggestions. Those in His Kingdom are the salt of the earth, the light of the world. His greatest commandment is for us to show love. There is no love in discrimination. God accepts everyone. His kingdom is for all and opens to all who will receive His love. This was true back in the first century and it still is true.

The fruits of the Spirit, the Beatitudes, love for all, these are what his Kingdom is about. On earth, his kingdom is a spiritual kingdom. His Kingdom resides within us. When we leave earth, we will go to live in his physical Kingdom called Heaven. Kingdom living is both spiritual and physical. The spiritual and physical work together, for what is done on earth, is done in heaven.

"And I will give to you the keys of the kingdom of heaven: and whatsoever thou shall bind on earth shall be bound in heaven: and whatsoever thou shall loose on earth shall be loosed in heaven" (Matthew 16:19).

Giving us the keys to the kingdom was not a onetime gift, it was meant to be one that carried on to all generations.

Where are you? Are you living in the kingdom, or are you looking at the kingdom from the outside?

Week 19-Wednesday

With Jesus everyone has a new beginning

1But Jesus went to the Mount of Olives. 2At dawn he appeared again in the temple courts, where all the people gathered around him, and he sat down to teach them. 3The teachers of the law and the Pharisees brought in a woman caught in adultery. They made her stand before the group 4and said to Jesus, "Teacher, this woman was caught in the act of adultery. 5In the Law Moses commanded us to stone such women. Now what do you say?" 6They were using this question as a trap, in order to have a basis for accusing him.

But Jesus bent down and started to write on the ground with his finger. 7When they kept on questioning him, he straightened up and said to them, "If any one of you is without sin, let him be the first to throw a stone at her." 8Again he stooped down and wrote on the ground.

9At this, those who heard began to go away one at a time, the older ones first, until only Jesus was left, with the woman still standing there. 10Jesus straightened up and asked her, "Woman, where are they? Has no one condemned you?"

11"No one, sir," she said.

"Then neither do I condemn you," Jesus declared. "Go now and leave your life of sin." (John 8:1-11)

Jesus did not focus His message on sin. He took people where they were at, not emphasizing their past mistakes. With Jesus, everyone had a new beginning. His approach was to teach love, love of God, and love of neighbor and everyone was a neighbor. His emphasis was on the need to care and to be concerned for God, for others and for all of God's creation. It was a positive message about love and relationship.

Jesus spoke in very down to earth parables about life, His values, and His vision of what our life could be. He preached a message of hope and freedom and salvation. He gathered thousands of people into a new community, a community in which there would be no vestige of the complex structure of laws, prohibitions, and rituals that had so burdened their lives. Setting people free was part of His main goal. Bringing people back to His Father's family was part of His gift to us.

Jesus realized this life he was sharing was fragile and easily shattered, so He gave his apostles the authority to reconcile those who had drifted or damaged their friendship with God. He also gave His disciples a food, which would nourish the divine life within them. He promised His followers that when they accepted His friendship, He and His Father would come and live within them.

The gift of God's living within us is the basis for the natural growth of the divine life received in baptism, except in many cases the relationship is not nourished. The intimacy with God was the source of Jesus' own strength in His humanity. It flowed from the rich prayer life that He nourished constantly. This is the secret to intimacy with God. We must maintain constancy in prayer, because it develops

within the soul a communion and a sharing of thoughts and feelings between the soul and God.

On earth, Jesus tried to help people understand that God knows our weakness and our efforts. He understands our struggling, our pain, and our determination to do better. As long as we are sensitive to the pain and loneliness of others, and reach out to heal, our own sins, as many as they may be, will be forgiven. This is the Good News! Share the good news with someone you love.

Week 19-Thursday

Jesus did not leave us alone

15"If you love me, you will obey what I command. 16And I will ask the Father, and he will give you another Counselor to be with you forever—17the Spirit of truth. The world cannot accept him, because it neither sees him nor knows him. But you know him, for he lives with you and will be[a] in you. 18I will not leave you as orphans; I will come to you. 19Before long, the world will not see me anymore, but you will see me. Because I live, you also will live. 20On that day you will realize that I am in my Father, and you are in me, and I am in you. 21Whoever has my commands and obeys them, he is the one who loves me. He who loves me will be loved by my Father, and I too will love him and show myself to him." (John 14:15-21)

If Jesus had stayed on earth, his physical presence would have limited the spread of the gospel, for physically he could be in only one place at a time. After his ascension, he would be spiritually present everywhere through the Holy Spirit. The Holy Spirit was sent so God would be with and within his followers after Jesus returned to heaven. His Spirit would comfort them, guide them to know his truth, remind them of Jesus' words, give them the right words to say, and fill them with power.

Jesus instructed his disciples to witness to people of all nations about him. However, they were told to wait first for the Holy Spirit. God had important work for them to do for Him, but they had to wait until they were given the strength and wisdom by the power of his Spirit.

The Spirit marks the beginning of the Christian experience. We cannot belong to Christ without his Spirit; we cannot be united to Christ without his Spirit; we cannot be adopted as his children without his Spirit; we cannot be in the body of Christ except by baptism in the Spirit. The Spirit is the power of our new lives. He begins a lifelong process of change as we become more like Christ. When we receive Christ by faith, we begin a personal relationship with God. The Holy Spirit works in us to help us become more like Christ.

Week 19-Friday

We have nothing to fear, God is with us.

"31What, then, shall we say in response to this? If God is for us, who can be against us? 32He who did not spare his own Son, but gave him up for us all—how will he not also, along with him, graciously give us all things? 33Who will bring any charge against those whom God has chosen? It is God who justifies. 34Who is he that condemns? Christ Jesus, who died—more than that, who was raised to life—is at the right hand of God and is also interceding for us. 35Who shall separate us from the love of Christ? Shall trouble or hardship or persecution or famine or nakedness or danger or sword? 36As it is written:

"For your sake we face death all day long; we are considered as sheep to be slaughtered." 37No, in all these things we are more than conquerors through him who loved us. 38For I am convinced that neither death nor life, neither angels nor demons, neither the present nor the future, nor any powers, 39neither height nor depth, nor anything else in all creation, will be able to separate us from the love of God that is in Christ Jesus our Lord." (Romans 8:31-39)

If God is at the center of our lives, we have nothing to fear from the outside world. We must know in our hearts that God is always with us and that God loves us unconditionally. However, we need to have faith in God's love in order to move forward on our Christian walk. We must be able to moment by moment surrender our wills and our lives to God and love one another as He loves us. Through the power of the Holy Spirit, we are reminded that we are deeply loved and totally accepted in that love and that we will never be left alone or abandoned. Jesus tells us that we are significant.

Love was the main message of Jesus. He loves us unconditionally, just as we are, with no strings attached to that love. God's love is personal. He knows each of us personally and calls us to join in friendship with him personally. God never gives up on us or abandons us, but continually calls us to a loving relationship with Him.

If we recognize that God is always with us, we have no need to fear.

Week 19-Saturday

Why do you worry? Why are you afraid?

Jesus asks us two questions: "Why do you worry?...Why are you afraid?" (Lk. 12:26 ; Mk. 8:26a)

The answer to the first question of Jesus seems almost trite—"Why do you

worry?" We want to say, "Do you KNOW what's going on here?" Yet in our hearts we know the truth that Jesus is trying to teach: for all our worry, we can't add one minute to our lifespan—in fact modern medicine tells us just the opposite: our worry in fact may actually take years of our lifespan. However, how do we cope with the temptation to worry? The answer to coping with worry is the answer to Jesus' second question:

We look at Jesus' second question here: "Why are you afraid?" and we recognize truth: We worry because we are afraid! We do not have to be afraid, because Jesus is with us! If Jesus is in our boat, we can survive any storm. That too seems trite, but we can deepen our faith in Jesus' saving presence by practicing that faith—turning over our worries to Jesus because we believe that he cares, and he can direct everything for our good. We can actually work on deepening our faith in the presence of Jesus with us, even if he is asleep in the boat.

Jesus keeps asking us: "Why do you worry? Why are you afraid?" because he wants two-way communication with us. Our worries are like cell phones we carry around but never use. I challenge you today: Every time you start worrying, "turn it over" and make the call to Jesus!

Every time you start stressing over a hectic schedule, a wedding coming up in the family, an obligation you can't meet, a sense of failure or inadequacy, "turn it over" and make the call to Jesus, who keeps asking: Why do you worry? Why are you afraid?

As we learn to do this, with all the big and little worries that fill our days, we will be building communication towers that can link Sunday to Sunday, pulling Sunday faith into Monday worries and Tuesday fears, pulling worship into daily life…We can also develop and deepen our love for Jesus, for as the 1st

Letter of John reminds us, "Perfect love casts out fear." The more our love for God grows, the easier it will be to entrust whatever worries us to God. Reading Scripture—even for five minutes a day—can help here. Try spending a month with Isaiah 43 or John 15, or some of the gospel passages. I can almost guarantee that your love for and trust in God and Jesus will deepen.

Week 19-Sunday

Jesus is our Compassonate Shephard

36When he saw the crowds, he had compassion on them, because they were harassed and helpless, like sheep without a shepherd. 37Then he said to his disciples, "The harvest is plentiful, but the workers are few. 38Ask the Lord of the harvest, therefore, to send out workers into his harvest field." (Matthew 9:36-38)

It is sometimes difficult for us to appreciate the depth of Jesus' emotions. We experience hurt and pain when others suffer. So did Jesus. However, for him, compassion went so much deeper. The Greek word used for compassion in the scriptures, describes powerful feelings from deep within one's inner being. What was it that aroused such feelings in Jesus? It was the tragic spiritual condition of his people. He looked at the crowds following him; he compared them to harassed, helpless sheep without a shepherd. The compassion felt by Jesus lead him to action. He ministered to the people both physically and spiritually.

Doesn't this sound a bit like our generation? In these troubled times, it appears that a great many of us are spiritually bankrupt. Doesn't it seem that we are a bunch of lost sheep looking for a shepherd.

It is time that we slow down our fast-paced lives, quiet ourselves, and listen for the voice of our shepherd. Jesus is our shepherd; we just need to learn to recognize his voice calling out to us. He is always there.

Week 20-Monday

"I am the Lord's servant," Mary answered

26In the sixth month, God sent the angel Gabriel to Nazareth, a town in Galilee, 27to a virgin pledged to be married to a man named Joseph, a descendant of David. The virgin's name was Mary. 28The angel went to her and said, "Greetings, you who are highly favored! The Lord is with you."

29Mary was greatly troubled at his words and wondered what kind of greeting this might be. 30But the angel said to her, "Do not be afraid, Mary, you have found favor with God. 31You will be with child and give birth to a son, and you are to give him the name Jesus. 32He will be great and will be called the Son of the Most High. The Lord God will give him the throne of his father David, 33and he will reign over the house of Jacob forever; his kingdom will never end."

34"How will this be," Mary asked the angel, "since I am a virgin?"

35The angel answered, "The Holy Spirit will come upon you, and the power of the Most High will overshadow you. So the holy one to be born will be called[a] the Son of God. 36Even Elizabeth your relative is going to have a child in her old age, and she who was said to be barren is in her sixth month. 37For nothing is impossible with God."

38"I am the Lord's servant," Mary answered. "May it be to me as you have said." Then the angel left her. (Luke 1:26-38)

Even though we recognize Mary as the mother of Jesus, the mother of God, I think we forget how brave she was to take on the magnitude of God's will. It could not have been easy for her, given the times in which she lived. She trusted in God unconditionally. She truly was a servant of the Lord. It was absolutely correct for Mary to have trusted in God, because throughout her trials, especially the birth of Jesus and his death on the cross, God remained with her. She allowed God to be her strength and her comforter. She said "yes" to God and God did not disappoint her.

It is good for us to remember that when we say "yes" to God, the road we travel is not without its share of heartbreak, or sorrow. However, when we walk the road of God's will, God is there to be our strength, our comforter, our savior. We may travel the more difficult road, but our rewards for doing this far outweigh any bad things that may happen along the way.

We must trust God as Mary did, and say, "I am the Lord's servant."

Week 20-Tuesday

God has things under control

22Then Jesus said to his disciples: "Therefore I tell you, do not worry about your life, what you will eat; or about your body, what you will wear. 23Life is more than food, and the body more than clothes. 24Consider the ravens: They do not sow or reap, they have no storeroom or barn; yet God feeds them. And how much more valuable you are than birds! 25Who of you by worrying can add a single hour to his life. 26Since you cannot do this very little thing, why do you worry about the rest.

27"Consider how the lilies grow. They do not labor or spin. Yet I tell you, not even Solomon in all his splendor was dressed like one of these. 28If that is how God clothes the grass of the field, which is here today, and tomorrow is thrown into the fire, how much more will he clothe you, O you of little faith! 29And do not set your heart on what you will eat or drink; do not worry about it. 30For the pagan world runs after all such things and your Father knows that you need them. 31But seek his kingdom, and these things will be given to you as well." (Luke 12:22-31)

Jesus knew that people can easily get caught up in worrying about having enough of the essential elements of life; food, clothing, and shelter. If you are worrying about things, you will not have very much energy to think about God. I think the point Jesus was making is that worry does not change anything. He pointed out that God takes care of all creation. Plants and animals do not have to think about their needs because God supplies food for them and makes them grow. He will take care of you as well because he loves you more than anything else in his creation.

So, do not waste your time worrying about stuff. Do not worry about a future that may not happen. Spend that time and energy trusting in God and growing your faith in God's caring and concern for you. If you Let God be the focus of your life, you will not have time to worry. Do not forget that God has things under control.

Week 20-Wednesday

What does it mean to worship?

21Jesus declared, "Believe me, woman, a time is coming when you will worship the Father neither on this mountain nor in Jerusalem. 22You Samaritans worship what you do not know; we worship what we do know, for salvation is from the Jews. 23Yet a time is coming and has now come when the true worshipers will worship the Father in spirit and truth, for they are the kind of worshipers the Father seeks. 24God is spirit, and his worshipers must worship in spirit and in truth." (John 4:21-24)

Worship is described as a response to who God is. Therefore, when you understand in your heart that God is, how much he loves you, and what his plan is for the future, your response to that becomes your worship. Worship is personal, so you can certainly do it alone; you do not have to wait until Sunday morning rolls around to worship God. However, worshiping with other people is important too, because it is an encouragement to others. It binds you together with other believers as sisters and brothers in God's family.

Jesus spent private time in prayer and conversation with his father, but his ministry was one of bringing people together in community. Both elements are important. Just as you love to have a private conversation with a dear friend or loved one, so should be your private time with God. In addition, isn't it great to have a party, to celebrate something within your community of friends and loved ones? Worshiping God in community should be a celebration. It should be a gathering of people who come together to celebrate God's love and goodness; to thank God for all he has given us. It should be a gathering of people who share their love for God. Gather together this Week not because you are supposed to, but because you want to share your love for God with others.

Week 20-Thursday

Finding Courage in Prayer

39"Jesus went out as usual to the Mount of Olives and his disciples followed him. 40On reaching the place, he said to them, "Pray that you will not fall into temptation." 41He withdrew about a stone's throw beyond them, knelt down and prayed, 42"Father, if you are willing, take this cup from me; yet not my will, but yours be done." 43An angel from heaven appeared to him and strengthened him. 44And being in anguish, he prayed more earnestly, and his sweat was like drops of blood falling to the ground." (Luke 22:39-44)

Courage is not always easy because it is not always popular. Courage is not so much about not being afraid, it involves the wisdom to know the difference between right and wrong and then acting upon that wisdom by doing what is right even if you are standing alone. No one likes to feel alone. The thing is, you really are not alone.

The Holy Spirit lives within you. He will give you the wisdom to make the right decisions. He will give you the courage to follow through on them. Jesus courageously faced his own death, but he was not alone. He prayed that he would have the courage to die. Now hopefully we will not have to pray for courage to die as Jesus did, but we may need the courage to die to those problems that keep us prisoner such as addictions, anger, or sorrow.

We pray to have the strength to face these deaths with courage, knowing that God is there with us. If we pray for courage, God will help us through our troubled times and our own deaths.

Week 20-Friday

How do we sacrifice?

"12My command is this: Love each other as I have loved you. 13Greater love has no one than this that he lay down his life for his friends. 14You are my friends if you do what I command. 15I no longer call you servants, because a servant does not know his master's business. Instead, I have called you friends, for everything that I learned from my Father, I have made known to you. 16You did not choose me, but I chose you and appointed you to go and bear fruit—fruit that will last. Then the Father will give you whatever you ask in my name. 17This is my command: Love each other." (John 15:12-17)

There is a socially acceptable level of giving to those in need and that is what many people live by. They give the leftovers of their time and money, or they give only when it is convenient. However, Jesus said that is not good enough. His example of giving is the standard. He left the glory of heaven to come to earth and become a servant to the very people who would one day kill him. That is real sacrifice.

Jesus sacrifice was not about money, it is really about love. I guess that we have to ask ourselves what do we sacrifice. I am sure that all parents will say that they sacrifice for their children. We sacrifice for our friends in need. That is all good and should continue. However, is that the extent of our sacrifice? Jesus said that it was not enough to be good to those who love you; you must be good to those who are not good to you. That is not easy to do. However, as Christians, we are called to love our enemies. Love is an outward sign of Christianity. "They will know we are Christians by our love." Love and sacrifice go together. What are you willing to do for those we love, even if they do not love us in return? Something to think about.

Week 20-Saturday

The Message of God's Love

3"Neither this man nor his parents sinned," said Jesus, "but this happened so that the work of God might be displayed in his life. 4As long as it is day, we must do the work of him who sent me. Night is coming, when no one can work. 5While I am in the world, I am the light of the world."

6Having said this, he spit on the ground, made some mud with the saliva, and put it on the man's eyes. 7"Go," he told him, "wash in the Pool of Siloam" (this word means Sent). So the man went and washed, and came home seeing." (John 9:3-7)

God never gets distracted from his plan. His plan from the beginning of time has been to have a personal relationship with people, so God's work always centers on that. Jesus knew that his purpose on earth was to do God's work, and he did that every day with all his energy. He found fulfillment in doing that. Jesus wants the message of God's love and care to be spread throughout the earth, and he set a good example for that himself. He knows that we cannot do his work on our own that is why God's strength is so important. God's strength will help us to do the work he has for us in sharing his message.

The things we say and do can show others about God and how much he loves us. The longer we walk with God, the more ways he will show us how to be a part of his work. Just remember that we do not have to do his work through our own strength. God is the one who will give us the ability to do his work, and God will provide the help we need.

Week 20-Sunday

Jesus called us his friends.

15I no longer call you servants, because a servant does not know his master's business. Instead, I have called you friends, for everything that I learned from my Father, I have made known to you. 16You did not choose me, but I chose you and appointed you to go and bear fruit—fruit that will last. Then the Father will give you whatever you ask in my name". (John 15:15-16)

The friendship that Christians have with Jesus is absolutely amazing, especially when we realize that we can have a personal, intimate relationship with the Son of God, who is responsible for creating and upholding the universe. It's overwhelming to grasp the truth of what it means is to be a friend of Jesus Christ.

Real friendship looks at the heart, not just the "packaging." Genuine friendship loves for love's sake, not just, for what it can get in return. True friendship is both challenging and exciting. It risks, it overlooks faults, and it loves unconditionally, but it also involves being truthful, even though it may hurt. Genuine friendship, also called "agape" love, comes from Jesus. Jesus calls us his friends and he laid down his life for us.

A Concluding thought.

Become like little children

At that time, the disciples came to Jesus and asked, "Who is the greatest in the kingdom of heaven?"

2He called a little child and had him stand among them. 3And he said: "I tell you the truth, unless you change and become like little children, you will never enter the kingdom of heaven. 4Therefore, whoever humbles himself like this child is the greatest in the kingdom of heaven.

5"And whoever welcomes a little child like this in my name welcomes me. 6But if anyone causes one of these little ones who believe in me to sin, it would be better for him to have a large millstone hung around his neck and to be drowned in the depths of the sea.

Why would Jesus want us to become like little children? It could be that children are a great example of what humility is about. Children are simple, trusting, lowly, loving, and forgiving. Children are not complicated. Their thoughts are honest, their motives are pure.

Children are completely trusting of their parents. If they need anything, a shoulder to sleep on, a diaper changed, milk, or food, a hand to help them walk, arms to crawl into, they turn to their mommy or daddy with wide eyes, open arms, and complete trust. Obstacles may be in the way, but as long as they are holding onto the hand of a parent, they are totally confident that they will make it.

Children love discovering and learning! They have no problem saying, "help me," "teach me," or "love me."

They point to everything wanting to know what it means, wanting to touch it, and to experience it for themselves. In complete humility, they are open to whatever their parent is telling them.

Children live in the present moment. They are not making elaborate plans for the future. They do not have lofty expectations. Their desires are simple and now! They accept that sometimes the answer is "no." Little children live in a state of wonder and joy. They look forward to a new day when they wake up in the morning.

Isn't this how we need to be with our Heavenly Parent, to be completely trusting of God? No matter what happens during our day, we can trust that God is indeed taking care of us. When we learn to trust and we hold onto God's hand, we will discover that no obstacle is too big. We may need to take some huge deep breaths to release all of our fears, but that is what children do. They simply trust their parents, they put all their faith in the fact that their parents will be there for them in times of trouble. We need to trust that God will be there for us. We can have confidence in the fact that God loves us. We can have faith that God will never abandon us. We can always have hope because God is taking care of us. Have a simple, childlike belief and trust in God. God will never let us down. That is what Jesus was saying.

Do not ever forget that God loves you!

Peace and love,

Sue Provost